VISIT THE
LOUVRE

Paintings
Drawings
Sculptures
Objets d'art

Text by Valérie Mettais

art
lys :

Cover: Leonardo da Vinci, Portrait of *Lisa Gherardini del Giocondo*,
    known as *"La Gioconda"* or *"Monna Lisa"* (detail), c. 1503-1506.
    Oil on wood, 77 x 53 cm
Pages 8 and 9: Ieoh Ming Pei, the glass pyramid in the centre
    of the Napoleon courtyard, 1989
Page 11: The Louvre of Philippe Auguste, XII century:
    foundations of the fortress and towers

Editorial coordination: Denis Kilian
Graphic design and production: Martine Mène
Picture research: Karine Barou; PAO: Hervé Delemotte
Plans: Thierry Lebreton, Dominique Bissière
Make-up: Pierre Kegels

© Artlys, Versailles, 2005
ISBN 2-85495-253-7

Contents

4

The Louvre, palace of the muse

Hubert Robert, *The Long Gallery of the Louvre*, c. 1794-1796

"It is a matter of making a Museum out of the galleries of the Louvre; it is decided and, as Interior Minister, I am the organiser and supervisor of the project. [...] This Museum is to be an expansion of the great wealth which the nation possesses in drawings, paintings, sculptures and other monuments of art. As I conceive it, it should attract foreign visitors and focus their attention; it should nurture a taste for fine arts and serve as a school for artists; it should be open to everyone [...]. This will be a national monument, there will be no-one not entitled to enjoy it." In 1792, in the first year of the Republic, Roland thus laid down the principles of what would, on 27th July 1793, become the central Museum for the Arts. The Louvre of kings gave way to a museum destined for a brilliant future.

A ROYAL HERITAGE

Whilst it fell to the Revolution to have founded and organised a museum intended for all citizens, to fulfil this it was based on a design developed in the middle of the century and adopted in the reign of Louis XVI: in 1776, a commission had studied the project; making inventories, restoring, supplementing the royal collections through purchases, it had prepared the ground.

When, on 10th August 1793, the Museum was opened in the square Drawing-room and the Long Gallery [Grande Galerie] which connects the Louvre to the national Palace - the former Tuileries -, what did it hold? From the kings, it inherited impressive sets of paintings, drawings and statuaries: the collection of paintings of François I, and those of Louis XIV or Louis XVI abound with accounts of the Italian Renaissance - Raphaël or Leonardo and his *Gioconda* -, of works of artists from the XVII century, known as the Grand Siècle, of Flemish, Dutch and other masters. Created by Henri IV, the "Antiques Room" was a treasury on which the museum would draw. Not to mention the riches of the Academy of Painting and Sculpture.

Hubert Robert, *The Long Gallery of the Louvre*, c. 1794-1796

EXCITING THE ADMIRATION OF THE WORLD

To this royal legacy, the I Republic, soon followed by the Consulate in 1799, added its contribution: it seized the property of émigrés and took possession of that of the Church - hence the regalia, instruments of the coronation of kings kept at the Abbey of Saint-Denis - and collected the booty of its armies that were scouring Belgium, Germany or Italy. For the Louvre owed it to itself to be amongst the most magnificent. Symbol of the victory of the people over its tyrants, an example of the glory of France, "it will excite the admiration of the world", it was said.

Then it was the turn of the empire to make its mark: a year even before his coronation, in 1803, Napoleon Bonaparte gave his name to the museum. The campaigns waged throughout Europe brought back numerous works to Paris: two architects, Percier and Fontaine, redeveloped the rooms in order to accommodate collections that

had become fabulously rich. DISCOVERING OTHER CIVILIZATIONS
In 1815, it all collapsed. The restored monarchy regained the Tuileries
and took care of the museum left by its predecessors. Its first task
was to return almost all the works seized. Transfers, donations, acqui-
sitions would gradually fill the void thus created: formed under the
Revolution, the museum of French Monuments was closed in 1817
and its collections provided a wide choice of sculptures; the canvases
which Rubens painted for the Luxembourg gallery made an impressive start; in 1821, the *Venus of Milo* was offered to Louis XVIII. Six years
later, the "Charles X Museum" was set up.
Whilst the Louvre could then pride itself on its masterpieces of western
art, it still had to cater for other civilizations. Organised in 1826, the
"Egyptian division" was entrusted to Jean-François Champollion,
who bought the collections of the French and English Consuls in
Egypt; the digs conducted in 1843 by Paul-Émile Botta, the French
Consul in Mosul, excavated the palace of Sargon II in Khorsabad: the
"Assyrian Museum" was founded. The same spirit would guide the
II Republic; after renaming the Louvre the "Palace of the People" in
1848, it restored, decorated and set up a museum of Ethnography
- the future Museum of Mankind.

GIFTS, LEGACIES AND PURCHASES
While the Second Empire began with ambitious works - reuniting the
Louvre with the Tuileries -, the museum continued its redevelopments,
undertook inventories and catalogues, encouraged donations - those
of Charles Sauvageot in 1856 or Dr. La Caze in 1869 - and acquired huge
collections, such as that of the Marquis de Campana in 1863, including
thousands of Greek and Etruscan ceramics, Italian paintings, majolica...
1863 also saw the arrival of the *Victory of Samothrace*.
Many were those who, under the III Republic, would through legacies
and donations continue this enrichment of the museum's departments: Camondo, Thiers, Schlichting, Chauchard, Rothschild,
Caillebotte, Moreau-Nélaton and so many others.

OPERATION GRAND LOUVRE
By a decision taken in 1981 to assign the entire palace to the museum,
the end of the XX century is adding a chapter to the history of the
Louvre. Opened in several stages - the glass pyramid and the reception
structures in the Napoleon courtyard in 1989, the Richelieu Wing
where a new presentation of collections replaced the Ministry of
Finance in 1993, the Denon and Sully Wings in 1997 -, the Grand
Louvre is on the point of being completed.
An encyclopaedic museum with its seven departments - oriental
antiquities covering the Islamic section, Egyptian antiquities, Greek,
Etruscan and Roman antiquities, paintings, graphic arts, sculptures and
objets d'art -, a museum-palace with breathtaking riches, the Louvre
makes it possible to discover and encounter anything. Here it is, ready
to start a new life.∇

François Heim, *Charles X distributing Awards to
Artists at the Salon of 1824*, 1827.
"Salons" of exhibitions of works of contemporary artists
are also held at the Louvre

Eugène Delacroix, *Apollo victorious
over the serpent Python*, 1850-1851.
Appolo Gallery, decoration of the
central sectionof the ceiling ordered
under the II Republic

Ieoh Ming Pei's glass pyramid,
interior view

PHILIPPE AUGUSTE CHARLES V	FRANÇOIS I	HENRI II	HENRI IV	LOUIS XIII LOUIS XIV

1190

Philippe Auguste (1180-1223) encircles Paris with a rampart flanked by a fortress to the west: the Louvre (located where the south-west quarter of the Quadrangle currently lies).

1214

In the keep, known as the "Great Tower", are gathered together the treasury, the archives and the Crown's furniture repository.

1226-1270

In the reign of St Louis, a room intended as an audience and reception room is built into the west wing.

1365-1370

Charles V (1364-1380) sometimes resides at the Louvre. He instructs the architect Raymond du Temple to enlarge the castle.

1528

François I (1515-1547) decides to settle in Paris and takes up residence at the Louvre: he orders the keep to be demolished and has the apartments decorated.

1540

The king receives Charles the Fifth at the Louvre.

1546

He entrusts the working out of the plan to Pierre Lescot: to reconstruct the building in the Renaissance style; the external dimensions remain unchanged. The architect erects the "main body of a royal residence".

1548-1553

In the reign of Henri II (1547-1559), Lescot's wing is completed; it is decorated by Jean Goujon. Building of the King's pavilion [Pavillon du Roi].

1550

In the ground floor room of the new Henri II wing, known as the "ballroom", Goujon erects a musicians gallery.

1559-1574

Buildings south of the present-day Quadrangle.

1564-1574

The regent Catherine de' Medici entrusts to Philibert de l'Orme the building of her palace, situated outside Charles V's enclosure: the Tuileries.

1566

Building of the Small Gallery [Petite Galerie] which, to the west, encloses the garden extending between the Louvre and the rampart parallel to the river.

1594-1610

In the reign of Henri IV (1589-1610), the "grand design" of the Louvre is conceived. Louis Métezeau and Jacques II Androuet du Cerceau build the Long Gallery, known as the "Riverside gallery", 460 metres long, which connects the Louvre to the Tuileries. Completion of the Small Gallery, connected to Lescot's building. The surface area of the palace courtyard is increased fourfold. On the ground floor of the Long Gallery the "Antiques Room" is set up, housing the royal collections.

1608

Henri IV decides to lodge the "King's workmen" in the Long Gallery.

1610-1643

In the reign of Louis XIII, Jacques Lemercier builds the Sully pavilion, or Clock pavilion [Pavillon de l'Hor-loge], adjoining Lescot's wing.

1655-1656

The regent Anne of Austria (1643-1661) sets up her summer apartments on the ground floor of the Small Gallery; Giovanni Francesco Romanelli is responsible for the painted decoration.

1659-1664

Louis XIV (1643-1715) entrusts the building of the north and south wings of the Quadrangle to Louis Le Vau.

1661-1670

Having burned down, the Kings' Gallery, on the 1st floor of the Small Gallery, is rebuilt by Le Vau and decorated by Charles Le Brun. The Tuileries are extended north by Le Vau and François d'Orbay; Le Nôtre designs the gardens.

The Louvre of Philippe Auguste, XII century: foundations of the fortress and towers

The Louvre of Charles V. Maître de Saint-Germain-des-Prés, *Pietà de Saint-Germain-des-Prés* (detail), c.1500

Pierre Lescot and Jean Goujon, south-west wing of the Quadrangle, 1548-1553

Louis Metezeau, eastern section of the "Riverside gallery", 1595-1607

Jacques Lemercier and Jacques Sarazin, Clock Pavilion, façade looking onto the Quadrangle, 1640

LOUIS XIV LOUIS XV	FROM LOUIS XVI TO THE CONSULATE	NAPOLEON I RESTORATION II REPUBLIC	NAPOLEON III	XX CENTURY XXI CENTURY

1667-1670
The east wing and its façade are built by Claude Perrault and Louis Le Vau; the Colonnade will be completed in 1812.

1678
Louis XIV leaves the Louvre and takes up residence at Versailles. Some four hundred items from the royal collection of paintings are kept at the Louvre: they form the beginnings of a semi-public museum.

1725
The annual exhibitions of the Royal Academy of Painting and Sculpture are held in the square Drawing-room or Salon: these "Salons" will be organised until 1848.

1750
In the reign of Louis XV, the plan is formed to open a museum and to show the collections in the Long Gallery. It is abandoned for lack of money.

1776
In the reign of Louis XVI (1774-1791), the Comte d'Angiviller, Supervisor of the king's Buildings, looks into the creation of a "museum"; in 1784, he appoints Hubert Robert "keeper" of the paintings.

1789
The people install Louis XVI in the Tuileries, which has become the "national Palace".

1791-1792
The royal collections become national ones. Works are seized from religious institutions and from émigrés. The revolutionary armies will bring back as booty works taken from all over Europe.

27th july 1793
Decree of the I Republic founding the central Museum of Arts, opened on 10th August.

1800
Bonaparte, the First Consul, occupies the Tuileries.

1803
The Museum becomes the "Napoleon Museum".

1806-1808
Napoleon I (1804-1815) entrusts to Charles Percier and Pierre Fontaine the building of the triumphal arch, the Arc de Triomphe du Carrousel, which marks the entrance to the Tuileries courtyard.

1810-1814
Construction of the north gallery along the rue de Rivoli.

1815
Under the Restoration, most of the works requisitioned are returned.

1826
Creation of an "Egyptian division" under the direction of Jean-François Champollion.

1827
Building of new rooms called the "Charles V Museum".

1838
Louis-Philippe's "Spanish Museum".

1847
Opening of the "Assyrian Museum".

1848
The II Republic decrees completion of the Louvre, named "Palace of the People".

1852-1857
Napoleon III (1852-1870) undertakes the construction of the "New Louvre", which he entrusts to Ludovico Visconti and then to Hector Lefuel; the Louvre and the Tuileries are joined together.

1861-1870
Lefuel rebuilds the west section of the Long Gallery and the Pavillon de Flore, decorated by Carpeaux. Construction of the wicket gates of the Carrousel.

1871
Under the Commune, the museum is run by a conservatory of artists. May: fire devastates the Tuileries, ruins not pulled down till 1883.

1929
Start of the reorganisation of the collections.

1953
The so-called Estruscan Room is decorated with medallions by Georges Braque.

1981
François Mitterand decides to assign the spaces occupied by the Ministry of Finance to the museum. Start of the Grand Louvre project.

1989
Unveiling of the pyramid by Ieoh Ming Pei in the Napoleon courtyard, opening of the main entrance and reception structures. Following excavations, the remains of the medieval Louvre are uncovered.

1993
Opening of the Richelieu Wing: 22,000 square metres accommodating the collections from four departments. Opening of the Napoleon III apartments.

1995-1997
Redevelopment of the Denon and Sully Wings

2004
Reopering of the restored Apollon gallery

Early XXIᵉ century
Completion of the Grand Louvre.

Claude Perrault, Louis Le Vau and Charles Le Brun, Colonnade, eastern façade, 1667

Hubert Robert, *Plan to develop the Long Gallery*, 1796

Hippolyte Bellange, *An Inspection Day under the Empire, 1810*, 1862. In the background, the Arc de Triomphe du Carrousel and the Tuileries

Ange Tissier, *The Architect Visconti presents the Plans for the New Louvre to the Sovereigns*, 1866

Giuseppe De Nittis, *The Place du Carrousel, ruins of the Tuileries*, 1882

Ieoh Ming Pei, the glass pyramid in the centre of the Napoleon courtyard, 1989

A fortress

In 1190, Philippe Auguste "took the Cross" and departed for the Crusade in the Holy Land, leaving his kingdom and capital defenceless. So he ordered the "townsmen of Paris to encircle the city, which he loved greatly, with a perfect wall including strong towers and gates", relates the chronicler Rigord. This enclosure would, for the first time, unite both banks of the Seine, from the Latin Quarter on the Left Bank to the Les Halles quarter on the Right Bank; with ten gates and seventy-five towers, it covered more than two hundred and seventy hectares. To the west, on land with sandy soil, it was flanked by a fortress intended to protect the city from any enemy that might come up-river. The "Louvre" was born. The word has given rise to numerous etymological hypotheses: from *lowar*, "fortified castle" in Saxon and *lu para*, "wolf-hunting lodge" to *rubra*, "red" - in allusion to the colour of the land... At the centre of this fortress, a vast quadrilateral armed with ten towers and surrounded by a waterditch, was erected a cylindrical keep: more than thirty metres high, equipped with a drawbridge, supplied by a well and circled by a dry ditch, what was called the "Great Tower" housed the arsenal, a prison and a few dwellings. It would fall to Charles V, in the XIV century, to transform this stronghold into a residence: after equipping Paris with a new rampart which took in the Louvre and its surroundings, he opened mullioned windows, erected the frames of buildings and a monumental staircase, designed pleasure gardens... The citadel became a royal residence. It was the start of a long history.

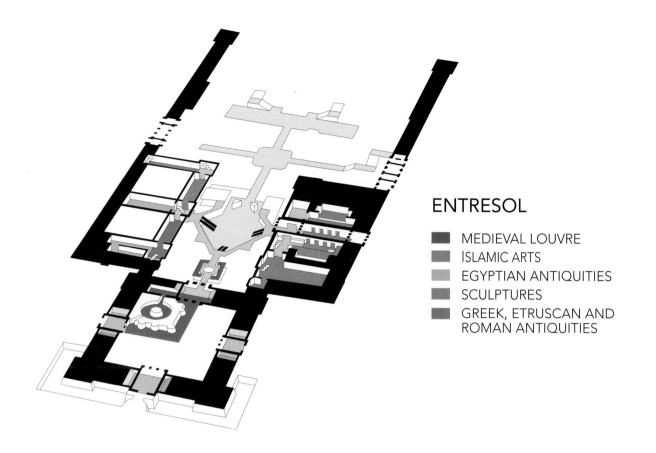

ENTRESOL

- MEDIEVAL LOUVRE
- ISLAMIC ARTS
- EGYPTIAN ANTIQUITIES
- SCULPTURES
- GREEK, ETRUSCAN AND ROMAN ANTIQUITIES

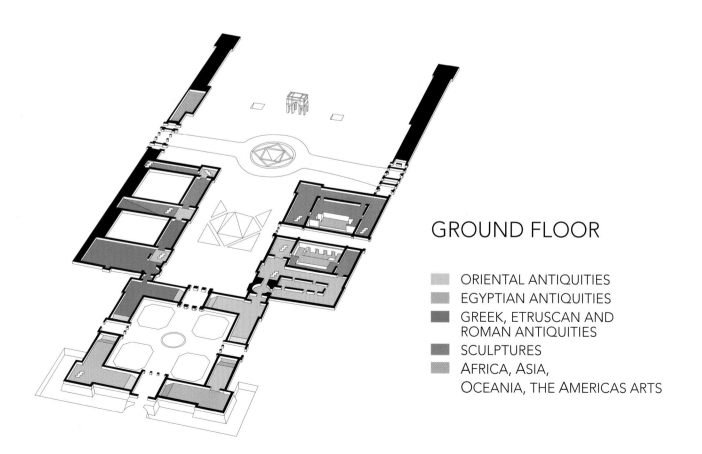

GROUND FLOOR

- ORIENTAL ANTIQUITIES
- EGYPTIAN ANTIQUITIES
- GREEK, ETRUSCAN AND ROMAN ANTIQUITIES
- SCULPTURES
- AFRICA, ASIA, OCEANIA, THE AMERICAS ARTS

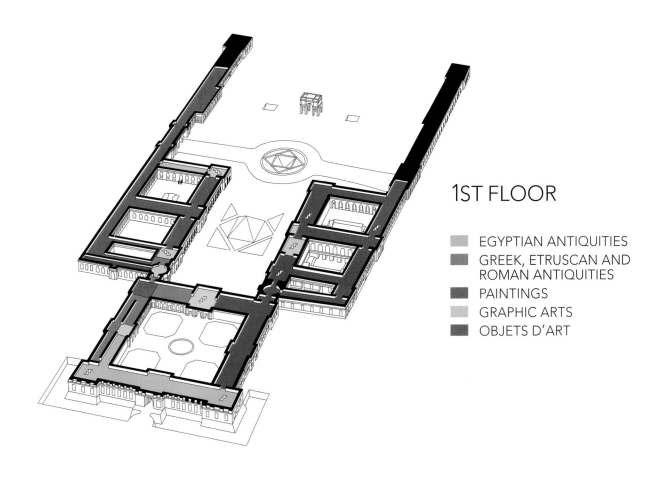

1ST FLOOR

- EGYPTIAN ANTIQUITIES
- GREEK, ETRUSCAN AND ROMAN ANTIQUITIES
- PAINTINGS
- GRAPHIC ARTS
- OBJETS D'ART

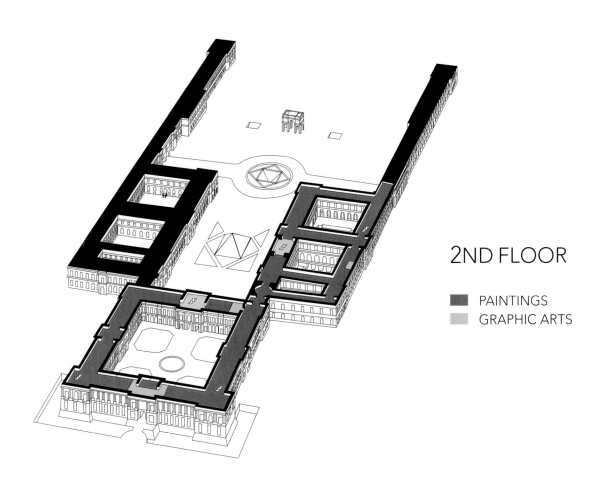

2ND FLOOR

- PAINTINGS
- GRAPHIC ARTS

These works are located in the Richelieu wing,
on the ground floor, in room 1a

Oriental antiquities

Stele of Vultures, detail of the "historical" side. Tello (ancient Girsu, Iraq),
c.2450 BC. Limestone, h: 170 cm
Ur-Nanshe Relief. Tello (ancient Girsu, Iraq), c.2500 BC.
Limestone, h: 40 cm

Builders and warriors

In lower Sumerian Mesopotamia, in that "land of two rivers" - the Tigris and the Euphrates - city-States began
to emerge during the III millenium BC: this was the birth of the city and society organized along hierarchi-
cal lines, the invention of writing and the development of sculpture, both placed in the service of power.
Whilst Ur-Nanshe, the founder of the I dynasty of Lagash, appears as a builder-king, a basket used to carry
bricks on his head, his grandson, Eannatum, is shown as a warrior-king; a stele recounts through text and
pictures his victory over the prince of Umma: on the "historical" side, he is commanding his troops as they
trample on the bodies of their enemies; on the "mythological" side, the god Ningirsu holds the prisoners
fast in a net.

These works are located in the Richelieu wing, on the ground floor, in room 1b

Oriental antiquities

Panel known as " Mari Standard ", c.2400 BC.
Shell and mother of pearl, h: 3.3 cm (figurines)
Statue of the administrator Ebih-il (detail). Mari (Syria), c.2400 BC. Alabaster,
eyes incrusted with shells and lapis lazuli, h: 52.5 cm

In the kingdom of Mari

On the banks of the Euphrates, the remains have been uncovered of an omnipotent city, Mari, which had a great palace and devoted many temples to its gods. There it was that the panels commemorating military conquests were lain, there the sovereigns and leading citizens placed their effigies, desiring in this way to offer up perpetual prayers to Ishtar, the great goddess of War. The administrator Ebih-il was one of the high-ranking individuals in the kingdom; he is shown in ceremonial dress, made from sheep's wool or goat's hair, the *kaunakes*, which could be worn as a skirt, as a shawl leaving the shoulder free or as a robe.

Oriental antiquities

Gudea with the gushing vase. Tello (ancient Girsu, Iraq),
c.2150 BC. Calcite, h: 62 cm
Prince Gudea reigned in Lagash, one of the last Sumerian dynasties
Statuette dedicated to the god Amurru for the life of Hammurabi. Larsa (Iraq),
c.1800 BC. Bronze and gold, h: 19.6 cm
Hammurabi's "code of law" (detail). Babylonian stele carried off as war booty to
Susa (Iran), c.1792-1750 BC. Basalt, h: 225 cm

Justice in Babylonia

Placing himself under the authority of Shamash, the Sun god and protector of Justice, Hammurabi,
sovereign of the I dynasty of Babylonia, had inscribed on a stele almost three hundred cases
that were debated and judged in his kingdom. All sorts of matters are mentioned: theft, murder,
adultery, contracts, debts and other personal and professional disputes. The sentences vary
according to the social rank of the victim: the freeman, then the *mushkenum,* belonging to a
lower class, lastly the slave.

These works are located in the Richelieu wing, on the ground floor, in room 4 and Sully wing, in room 12 a

Oriental antiquities

Grand capital showing bulls. Susa (Iran), audience room of the royal palace, c.520-500 BC. Limestone, h: 552 cm
Frieze of Archers. Susa (Iran), royal palace, c.500 BC.
Bas-relief in enamelled bricks, h: 183 cm (archers)
Winged androcephalous bull. Khorsabad (Iraq), courtyard of the palace of Sargon II, 713-706 BC. Gypseous alabaster, h: 440 cm
See double page overleaf

Assyrian empire…

In 1843, when the French consul in Mossoul began excavations at Khorsabad, he thought that he had uncovered the foundations of Nineveh, the last residence of the Assyrian sovereigns. But it turned out to be Dûr-Sharrukîn, the "fortress of Sargon", another capital of the empire. Built on a terrace, the palace covers ten hectares and has two hundred courtyards and halls; bas-reliefs adorn the walls for over two kilometres, finally the main gate is guarded by bulls with human bodies and wearing the sacred tiara. Several years later, an Assyrian Museum was opened at the Louvre.

… Persian Empire

Many were the capitals of the huge Persian Empire, which stretched from the Mediterranean to the Indus: Parsagades, and Ecbatana during the summer, Persepolis the Magnificent and Susa, the administrative and political centre, where the palace was built by Darius, a Persian prince belonging to the dynasty of the Achaemenides. Friezes of archers clothed in court robes, wearing bracelets and earrings, celebrate the glory of the armies. In the audience room, the columns are surmounted by bull-head capitals.

These works are located in the Richelieu wing,
on the entresol, in rooms 8 and 12

Islamic arts

Bowl known as " Baptistery of St Louis ", signed Muhammad ibn al-Zayn.
Syria or Egypt, Mameluke art, end of the XIII-start of the XIV century.
Hammered brass, chased and inlaid with silver, gold and black paste, h: 23.2 cm
Portrait of Shah 'Abbas I with one of his pages, signed Muhammad Qasim.
Iran, Sefevide art, 12th March 1627. Gouache and gold on paper, 27.5 x 16.8 cm
Peacock dish. Iznik (Turkey), Ottoman art, 1540-1555. Silicon ceramic
with decoration painted under glaze, diameter: 37.5 cm

The craftsemen of Islam

There is islam and there is Islam. It's all a matter of a capital letter... The former, the
"surrender to God", describes the religion preached by Mohammed in the VII century;
the latter would unite the peoples, from very diverse origins, who would share this
faith and form a civilization. Barely a century after the death of the prophet in 632, islam
stretched from Spain to India, became established in Egypt, Syria, Turkey, Iran... Taking
local traditions as its basis, it exhibits its originality through all types of art and techniques, metal, ceramic or miniature, affording pride of place to embellishment, the
stylization of forms, plant motifs or even to evoking the lives of princes.

Islamic arts

Large white dish with epigraphic decoration, known as the "Science Dish".
Khorasan or Transoxania (Iran), Xth-XIth century. Clay ceramic with slip decoration
under transparent glaze, diameter: 38.8 cm
Peacock clock, page from the *Book of knowledge of ingenious mechanical
devices* or *Automata,* written in the XIIIth century by the engineer, al-Jazari.
Egypt or Syria, 1354. Gouache with gold and silver highlights on paper,
40 x 28.2 cm
Celestial sphere, by the astrolabe maker, Yunus ibn al-Husayn. Baghdad (?), 1145.
Cast copper alloy, engraved and inlaid with silver, diameter: 16.5 cm

A taste for science

Arithmetic, music, geometry, astronomy, mechanics, optics and even medicine: no scientific discipline was left unexplored in the Islamic world. Continuing with and moving beyond Greek tradition, then imparting their knowledge to the West, scholars produced a multitude of treatises and designed instruments to observe the stars or study the universe. Immensely respected and broadly supported, science lay at the very heart of society, civilisation and religion. "Science, its taste is bitter at the beginning but, at the end, sweeter than honey", reads a Kufic inscription on a large white dish.

These works are located in the Richelieu wing, on the entresol, in rooms 8, 9 and 12

Islamic arts

Vase in the name of sultan al-Malik al-Nasir Salah al-Din Yusuf, known as the "Barberini Vase". Damascus or Aleppo, 1237-1260. Brass with repoussé decoration, engraved and inlaid with silver, h: 45 cm. In the XVIIth century, this vase was probably given to Pope Urban VIII Barberini

The Archangel Gabriel reveals Sura 8 (The Spoils) to the Prophet, page from the *Siyar-i Nabi (Life of the Prophet).* Manuscript written in the XIVth century in Egypt, copy ordered by Murad III, calligrapher Mustafa ibn Wali. Istanbul, 1594-1595. Pigments and gold on paper, 37.5 x 27.3 cm

Mosque lamp in the name of sultan Nasir al-Din Hasan. Egypt or Syria, 1347-1361. Blown glass decorated with enamel and gilt, h: 35.5 cm

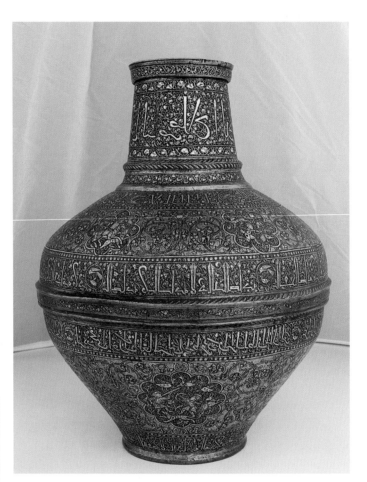

Calligraphy

Writing is everywhere, because writing is sacred: it was in Arabic that the prophet Mohammed received the divine revelation from Archangel Gabriel; it was this language, and hence this writing, which would be used to carry the message of the new religion. A symbol of Islam, calligraphy invades manuscripts and bookbinders, lamps and vases, architectural friezes and designs, written in black ink on paper and parchment, enamelled on glass and etched into metal. Triumphant and refined, it is an art that princes delighted in practising, and artists would often put their name to their work. Can there be anything nobler than to be a calligrapher?

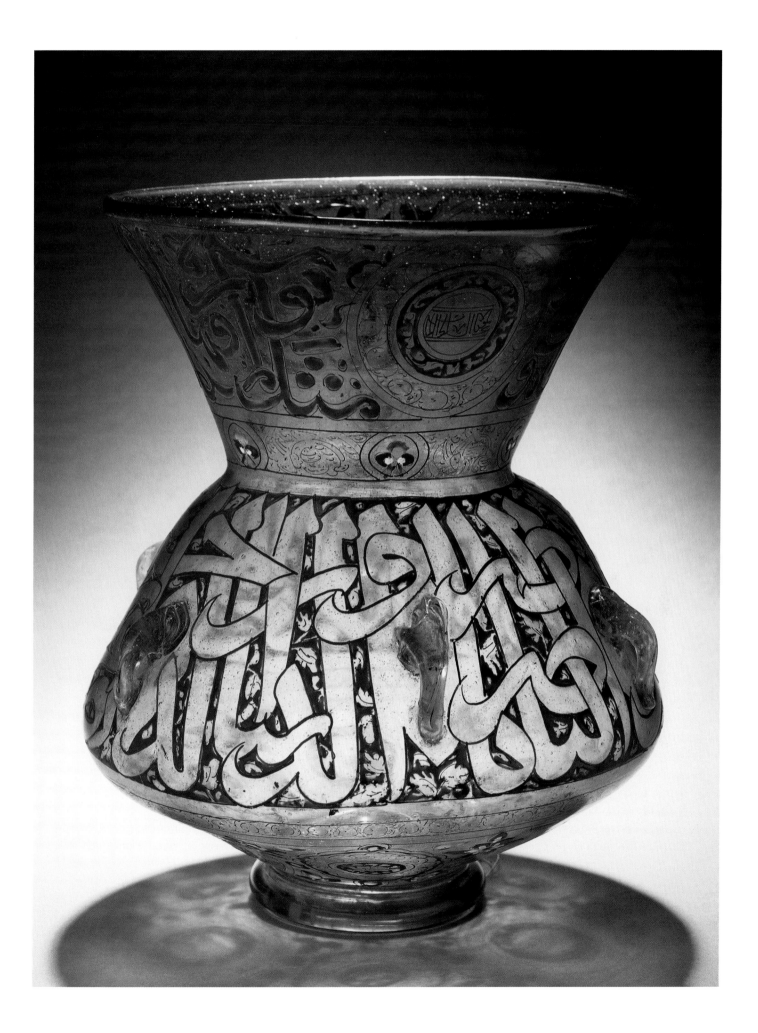

These works are located in the Richelieu wing,
on the entresol, in rooms 3 and 6

Islamic arts

Decoritive element. Egypt, IIth century Cypress wood, 67,5 x 18,1 cm
Pyxis in the name of al-Mughira, son of the caliph 'Abd al-Rahman III. Cordoba, 968. Elephant ivory sculpted and engraved, h: 15 cm
Lion perfume burner. Khorasan (Iran), XIth-XIIth century. Cast bronze with openwork decoration, engraved and inlaid with glass mosaic (?), 28,2 x 32 cm

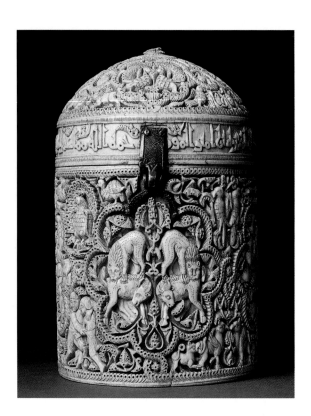

Animals and forms

Like plant motifs, animals feature frequently in decorations. Whether they are lifelike and anecdotal in their representation, be they part of the real or imaginary worlds, more often than not their forms are stylised. Stylisation involves exaggerating a line in order to emphasise a character, introduce movement, create unity: thus a lion stands on tapered legs, his triangular ears pricked up, big cats with raised hindquarters attack gazelles or a bird with an elongated neck opens a perfectly round eye.

This work is located in the Sully area,
on the 1st floor, in room 20

Egyptian antiquities

Dagger. Gebel el-Araq, Nagada civilization, c.3300-3200 BC.
Flint blade, haft made from the canine tooth of a hippopotamus, h: 25.5 cm
Bull palette. Nagada civilization, c.3150 BC.
Schist, h: 26.5 cm
Stele of the snake-king or the horus djet (detail). Saqqara, I Dynasty,
c.3100 BC. Limestone, h: 143 cm

Horus, the god of kings

Battles on land and sea, soldiers drowned and bound hand and foot, a bull crushing a man, and lions, ibexes, dogs and giraffes: these are the scenes conveyed on painted palettes laid in tombs, near the body, or in the temples. Images of war or animal representations, they bear witness to the existence of principalities on the banks of the Nile before the unification of Upper and Lower Egypt, governed by an absolute monarchical system. Then, Horus, the god of Light, son of Isis and Osiris, would be chosen to protect the land. He would give his name to the first sovereigns. On his funerary stele, the third pharaoh of the I dynasty inscribed his title, "The king (the Horus) Djet": above a *serekh*, a setting evoking a palace façade, stands the dynastic falcon; the snake illustrates the letter *dj* or the word *djet*.

These works are located in the Sully area,
on the 1st floor, in room 22

Egyptian antiquities

Stele of Nefertiabet. Giza, the princess's tomb, Old Kingdom, IV Dynasty,
c.2590 BC. Painted limestone, 37.5 x 52.5 cm
Scribe squatting. Saqqara, Old Kingdom, IV or V Dynasty,
c.2620-2350 BC. Painted limestone, eyes inlaid with rock crystal and alabaster and
encircled with copper, h: 53.7 cm

Writing, a privilege

Writing held a privileged place in ancient Egypt, for it was through it that the message of the Pharaoh was conveyed.
"Become a craftsman of language and you will triumph: the craftsman's language is the King's sword! Words are worth
more than any battle: one cannot catch a craftsman unawares", the sovereign Kheti would advise his son Merikarê. The
office of scribe, whether a simple copier or a high functionary, at that time enjoyed the highest consideration. It is
writing yet again which, endowed with magic powers, makes it possible for the deceased to have at his disposal all the
dishes and objects necessary for his existence in the Beyond.

Thes works are located in the Sully area,
on the entresol, in room 1

Egyptian antiquities

Lintel of Sesostris III: the king makes offerings of bread to Montou, the god of
War. Medamoud, Middle Kingdom, XII Dynasty,
1878-1843 BC. Limestone, h: 106 cm
Hippopotamus. Start of the Middle Kingdom, c.2000-1900 BC. Egyptian
"earthenware" (compressed grains of quartz covered with a glaze),
h: 12.7 cm
Great sphinx. Tanis, Middle Kingdom, XII Dynasty,
c.1850 BC. Pink granite, h: 183 cm

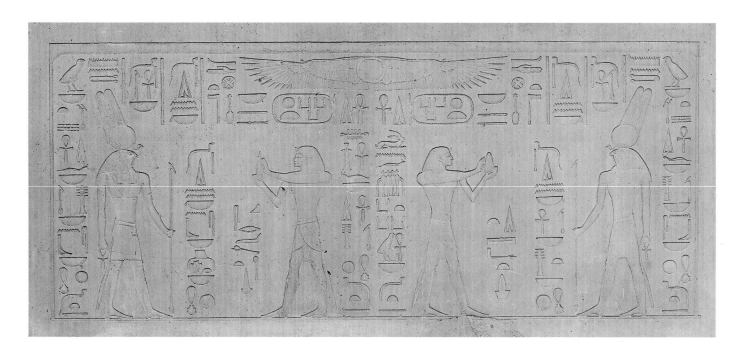

Presence of the pharaoh

Whether he takes the form of a sphinx, a recumbent lion with a man's head, or whether he appears with
realistic features presenting offerings to a god, the pharaoh is omnipresent, in all places and in all forms:
as a warrior, a praying figure, a prince hunting wildfowl or hippopotami in the marshes of the Nile... In this
way does he stamp with his presence and divine authority the temples and their surroundings, the procession
routes or the funerary buildings embellished with bas-reliefs and paintings.

These works are located in the Sully area,
on the 1st floor, in rooms 24 and 25

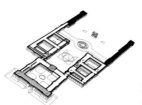

Egyptian antiquities

Statue of Nefertiti (?). Amarna, New Kingdom, XVIII Dynasty,
c.1365-1349 BC. Red sandstone, h: 29 cm.
Statuette of Akhenaten and Nefertiti. Amarna, New Kingdom, XVIII Dynasty,
c.1365-1349 BC. Painted limestone, h: 22.5 cm
"Swimming woman" spoon. New Kingdom, XVIII Dynasty,
c.1400 BC. Wood, L: 29 cm
Colossal statue of Akhenaten (detail). Amarna, New Kingdom, XVIII Dynasty,
c.1365-1349 BC. Painted sandstone, h: 137 cm

The beauty of Aten

Raised to power, Amenophis IV overturned the religious and political foundations of his kingdom.
He refused to worship Amon and preferred Aten, the sun disk, who dispensed air and light upon
earth. Henceforth the pharaoh would call himself "Akhenaten" - "He who serves the sun disk". He
left Thebes and built a new capital, Amarna. Ultimately, he dictated to his artists principles unheard
of until then: the pursuit of naturalism to show bodies with all their faults or in all their sensuality,
the expression of feelings, such as tenderness between man and wife.

These works are located in the Sully area, on the ground floor, in room 16

Egyptian antiquities

Scene of psychostasia the weighing of the heart (detail).
Book of the Dead. New Kingdom, XVIII Dynasty, c.1500-1400 BC.
Funerary papyrus
The goddess hathor and king Sety I. Valley of the Kings, tomb of Sety I,
New Kingdom, XIX Dynasty, c.1303-1290 BC.
Painted limestone, 226 x 105 cm

Sacred characters

"These characters so varied in form, often so contrary in their physical expression, are no less than signs which serve to record a regular series of ideas, express a fixed, continuous meaning and thus constitute true writing", wrote Champollion in 1824. The Egyptologist was able to discern the different functions of hieroglyphs: these are ideograms (showing an object, an action, an idea), phonograms (representing a sound, formed by two or more consonants) or determinatives (specifying the meaning of a term). The whole thing is without punctuation, capital letters or spaces between words.

These works are located in the Sully area,
on the ground floor, in room 14

Egyptian antiquities

Funerary stele of Taperet. XXII Dynasty, c.900-800 B C.
Painted wood, 31 x 29 cm
Sarcophagus of chancellor Imeneminet (coffin and lid) XXV - XXVI Dynasties,
c.700-600 BC. Stuccoed and painted wood, h: 188 cm

The life of the dead

Preparing oneself to live in the beyond was a basic preoccupation for all Egyptians. On the
sarcophaghi, stelae or the walls of the chambers are shown the rites of passage to be followed,
magic formulae, scenes of burial or resuscitation of the mummy, scenes of daily life after death,
prayers addressed to the deities - such as Ra-Horakhti, the "Sun at its zenith", with a falcon's
head bearing the disk. Not forgetting to place oneself under the protection of the eye of Horus.

These works are located in the Denon wing,
on the entresol, in room 2

Egyptian antiquities

Christ and father Mena. Baouît Monastery, VII century.
Tempera on wood, 57 x 57 cm
Funerary portrait of a young woman known as "Portrait of the Faiyum".
Antinoe, Romano-Egyptian art II century AD. (?).
Wax painting on wood

A conquered land

The Greeks called the inhabitants of the land of the Pharaohs *aiguptioi*. From this word came the term "Copt", which would describe the culture and writing of those Egyptians who became Christians. For the country would well and truly lose all independence. Conquered by Alexander in 333, it became Hellenic. When Octavius overcame Cleopatra at Actium in 31 BC, it was the property of the Roman Empire. Then it would be Byzantine, and finally Moslem in 641.

These works are located in the Denon wing,
on the entresol, in room 1

Greek antiquities

Statue of a woman, or the "Woman of Auxerre". Crete (?), Archaic Period, c.630 BC. Limestone, h: 75 cm
Fragment of female statuette. Cyclades Islands, Old Bronze Age, c.2700-2400 B.C. Marble, h: 18.5 cm
Head of a horseman, or the "Rampin horseman". Acropolis, Athens, Archaic Period, c.550-540 BC. Marble, h: 27 cm

Sculptors in the city

While, in the Greece of the Archaic Period, sculptors - like painters and potters - were respected because they were inventors, creators of forms, having received as gifts from the gods a precious ability and high degree of skill in technical mastery, they were also considered as simple craftsmen, occupied with manual tasks, hewing marble or casting bronze in a workshop, and working to order. Eager to enjoy the same consideration as that accorded to artists of the word, poets and philosophers, they would gradually begin to sign their works and to erect cultural statues on the Acropolis in Athens.

These works are located in the Sully area
on the ground floor, in room 7

Greek antiquities

Bowl in the shape of a drinking-cup in the "red-figured" style, ascribed to the painter of the Niobides.
Attic workshop, c.460 BC. Terracotta, h: 54 cm
Detail of the procession of the Panathenaea. Plaque from the frieze of the Parthenon. Acropolis, Athens, Classical Era, 438-431 BC.
Marble, 96 x 207 cm

The boldness of Athens

"Distinguished features are to be found, and there is no shortage of accounts to testify to our power and to offer us up to the admiration of all, now and in the future; we have no need of a Homer to glorify us, nor of anyone whose tones will charm for a while, but whose interpretations must suffer on account of the truth of the facts: we have compelled every sea and every land to draw back before our boldness, and everywhere we have left behind us undying monuments." When Pericles made this defence on behalf of Athens - which he would govern for fifteen years -, the Parthenon had just been finished. Town-planning, architecture, sculpture and painting: everything would go to prove the glory of the city.

These works are located in the Denon wing,
on the 1st floor

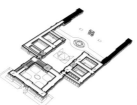

Greek antiquities

Statue of Victory. Samothrace, Hellenistic Era,
c.190 BC. Marble, h: 328 cm
Statuette of Victory. Myrina, Hellenistic Era, start of the II century BC.
Terracotta, h: 27.8 cm

The wings of the gods

Nike, the allegory for Victory, may be represented with wings unfurled and set upon ship's prow: for she celebrates a battle. But these wings are also the attribute of other divine forces which connect heaven to earth, gods to men and men to the Beyond: Iris, the personification of the rainbow, Hypnos, the god of Sleep, often accompanied by his brother, Thanatos, Aeolus, master of the Winds, followed by Boreas, god of the North Wind, and Zephyr, god of the Breeze or West Wind. Not forgetting Eros, the god of Love. As for the wings of Hermes, attached to his sandals, they allow this god of movement, and protector of merchants and thieves, to be the fastest of all the messengers.

These works are located in the Denon wing,
on the 1st floor

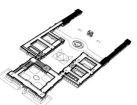

Greek antiquities

Combatant warrior, or the "Borghese gladiator". Antium, Hellenistic Era, c.100 BC. Marble, h: 157 cm
Combatant man. Asia Minor, Hellenistic Era, second half of the II century BC. Bronze, silver inlays for the eyes and copper inlays for the nipples, h: 25 cm
"Venus of Milo". Melos, Hellenistic Era, c.100 BC. Marble, h: 202 cm

Nudity of gods and men

Figures of heroes or statues of Aphrodite: Greek sculpture extols the nudity of the body. It does not always seem to have been so, Plato in the *Republic* written in the IV century BC tells: "It is not long since the Greeks thought it shameful and ridiculous that men allowed themselves to be seen totally naked, as most barbarian races still do now, and that when gymnastics were introduced first by the Cretans, and later by the Lacedaemonians, the witty men of the day had the opportunity of making fun of all these things, [...] But when in exercising they found that it was better to strip than to cover up that part of the body, then what had seemed ridiculous to the eye in nakedness disappeared in the face of reason showing what was best."

These works are located in the Denon wing,
on the ground floor, in room 18

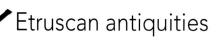

Etruscan antiquities

"**Sarcophagus of man and wife**". Cerveteri, c.510 BC.
Painted terracotta, h: 114 cm
Wall plaque, or "Campana plaque" (detail). Cerveteri, c.530-520 BC.
Painted terracotta, h: 118 cm

Cerveteri's man and wife

In XIX century, the director of the pawnshop in Rome was also an enlightened art lover who collected a fantastic set of Primitive paintings and antique works. But the Marquis de Campana committed a breach of trust, pledging his assets above their value. He was sent to the galleys; everything was confiscated and sold. By good fortune, his step-mother, Hortense Cornu, made use of her connections in France and sorted things out: Napoleon III turned the sentence into exile and bought most of the collection for the Louvre, particularly the funerary furniture brought to light at Cerveteri.

These works are located in the Denon wing,
on the ground floor, in room 23

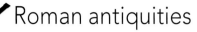

Roman antiquities

Census proceedings on the campus Martius (detail).
" Altar of Domitius Ahenobarbus ", decoration from the base of a statuary group.
Rome, end of the II century BC. Marble, 78 x 559 cm
Portrait of the emperor Hadrian. Rome, second quarter of the II century.
Bronze, h: 43 cm

The art of power

"Others will have greater skill for getting the breath of life to spring from bronze more fluidly and for more smoothly drawing forth from marble shuddering faces. But as for you, Roman, remember to impose your power upon nations. Your art is to decree the rules of peace, to spare the vanquished and subdue the vainglorious." Such was the advice conveyed in the *Aeneid* by Virgil, that poet who, in the reign of Augustus, placed himself in the service of imperial ideology.

These works are located in the Richelieu wing,
on the 2nd floor, in rooms 1, 3 and 6

French paintings

French school, *Portrait of John the Good*, c.1350. Tempera on wood, 60 x 44 cm
Jean Malouel, *Pietà*, or *La Grande Pietà ronde*, c.1400.
Tempera on wood, diameter: 64.5 cm
Jean Fouquet, *Portrait of Charles VII*, c.1445-1450. Tempera on wood,
85.7 x 70.6 cm

Painters' recipes

The techniques used by the "painters of popular pictures "[peintres ymagiers], as they were called in the Middle Ages, varied according to the studios: each one tried out his recipes and had
his secrets. Thus it was for painting in tempera. The pigments were earth-based, and based on
mineral oxides, animal or plant matter; black could be obtained from almond shells or burned
vine shoots, or even from lamp-black. These colours were ground with water, thinned, diluted.
Then leather glue was added, sometimes also wax or egg yolk mixed with vinegar; sometimes
it was combined with gum arabic, honey, fig-tree milk... The medium, planks of wood joined together, differed according to region: oak in the North, in France, Flanders and Holland, walnut south
of the Loire, lime in Germany, poplar in Italy...

LE TRESVICTORIEVX ROY·DE FRANCE ✦

CHARLES ✦SEPTIESME·DE·CE·NOM·

This work is located in the Richelieu wing,
on the 2nd floor, in room 4

French paintings

Enguerrand Quarton, *Pietà de Villeneuve-lès-Avignon*, c.1455.
Tempera on wood, 163 x 218 cm

Lamentations

By inscribing the names of the sacred characters within each halo, the painter doubtless enabled the observer to recognize them. But it above all gave him the chance of pronouncing these words, making them out little by little, with difficulty. Here we have the Virgin of Pietà bearing the body of her son on her lap, here is a Lamentation which brings together St John the Evangelist, the Magdalen and a donor. This lamentation is answered by the phrase engraved at the top, against the gold background - where celestial Jerusalem is shown -, taken from the first poem of the Lamentations of Jeremiah: "You who pass by, look and see: is there any sorrow like the sorrow that torments me." The sorrow of the prophet is united with that of the mother of Christ.

These works are located in the Richelieu wing, on the 2nd floor, in room 10

French paintings

Fontainebleau school, *Gabrielle d'Estrées and one of her sisters in the bath,* c.1595. Oil on wood, 96 x 125 cm
Fontainebleau school, *Diana the Huntress,* c.1550. Oil on wood, 191 x 132 cm

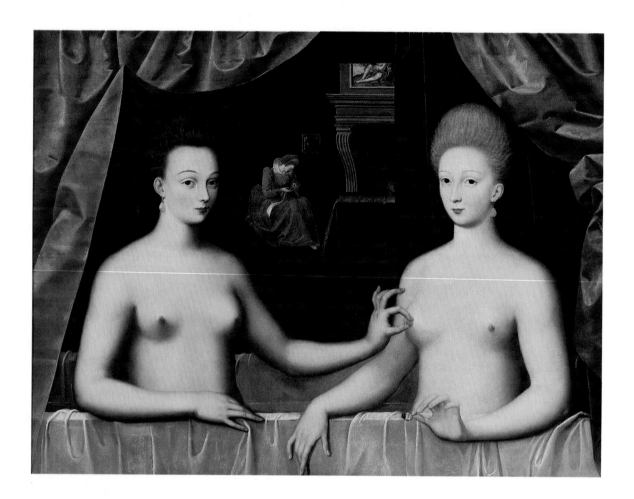

The breast uncovered

The favourites of the Renaissance lent their nakedness to the aesthetics of the artists of Fontainebleau. One of them, doubtless Diane de Poitiers, the mistress of Henry II, conceals herself behind the slender charms of a huntress goddess. The other, Gabrielle d'Estrées, the beloved of Henry IV, shows off her ring, a sign of a love bond, whilst her sister is pinching her nipple: for Gabrielle is going to be a mother - a woman in the background is preparing the babyclothes for the king's child. A symbol of rest and gentleness or a sign of motherhood, the breast also places women between two states: "Uncover then, wife and mother / This breast over which we quarrel. / Nature places there a button, / One is for the son, the other for the father", runs a poem.

This work is located in the Sully area,
on the 2nd floor, in room 28

French paintings

Georges de La Tour, *The Cheat (with the Ace of Diamonds),* c.1635.
Oil on canvas, 107 x 146 cm

Game of cards, dance of hands

"Gambling, wine and Women / Cause us to lose our souls", it was said at the time of La Tour.
Indisputably, the XVII century was the high-point of gambling: a certain La Marinière published
the "Maison académique des jeux", the first compilation of rules. Very quickly, people were taken
up with issues of morality for was not gambling above all a sin? A short booklet offered reflection on the matter: *A Christian issue relating to gambling, addressed to the ladies of Paris by
Théotime - to know whether a person given over to gambling is able to save themselves and
principally women.* But gambling also involves cheating, sleight of hand and fleeting looks, the
presence of an accomplice. Once again, the XVII century broke new ground in the field:
henceforth the term "to cheat" would refer to a practice employed in games.

These works are located in the Sully area,
on the 2nd floor, in room 28

French paintings

Georges de La Tour, *The Repentant Magdalen,* c.1640-1645.
Oil on canvas,128 x 94 cm
Georges de La Tour, *St Joseph the Carpenter,* c.1640.
Oil on canvas, 137 x 102 cm

The emergence of the light

To position the flame of a candle in the centre of the composition so that it causes a character to emerge from the darkness or, conversely, so that it reveals only a few details is the quest of the painter: here we see the profile of a woman, a skull, books on a table, the brow of an old man or the slender hand of a child, here is the repentance of the Magdalen, the work of Joseph. Thus is devotion bound up with the shadows and the emergence of the light.

This work is located in the Sully area,
on the 2nd floor, in room 29

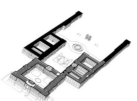

French paintings

Louis or Antoine Le Nain, *Family of peasants indoors,*
c.1640-1645. Oil on canvas, 113 x 159 cm

Painters of a reality

In the middle of XIX century, people had forgotten the very name of the Le Nain brothers when a writer and socialist critic, Champfleury, defender of realism, friend of Daumier and of Courbet, discovered them and created their legend: the three brothers, Louis, Antoine and Mathieu, painters from Laon established in Paris, are said to have met with little success, their representations of humble peasants in this France of the Old Regime having been judged too "realistic". But the Le Nains' work was a different matter altogether. From their studio in Saint-Germain-des-Prés came highly prized paintings: peasant subjects painted with restraint and monumentality, but also society portraits, altar-pieces and other mythological scenes.

These works are located in the Richelieu wing,
on the 2nd floor, in room 14

French paintings

Nicolas Poussin, *The Rape of the Sabine Women*, c.1637-1638.
Oil on canvas, 159 x 206 cm
Nicolas Poussin, *The Poet's Inspiration*, c.1630. Oil on canvas, 182 x 213 cm
Nicolas Poussin, *Self-portrait*, 1650. Oil on canvas, 98 x 74 cm

"I have been careless about nothing"

The man who, on the matter of his art, said: "I have been careless about nothing", stated in a letter dated 1st March 1665, a few months before his death, a number of his principles. What is imitation in art? "It is imitation made with lines and colours on some surface of all one sees beneath the sun, its aim is delight." And how should one paint? "One must begin with the arrangement, then with embellishment, adornment, beauty, grace, vivacity, costume, verisimilitude and discernment throughout. These last are virtues innate in the painter and cannot be learned."

These works are located in the Richelieu wing,
on the 2nd floor, in room 15

French paintings

Claude Gellée, or Lorrain, *The Village Fête*, 1639.
Oil on canvas, 103 x 135 cm
Claude Gellée, or Lorrain, *Seaport in the Setting Sun*, 1639.
Oil on canvas, 103 x 137 cm

Landscape and history

The "hierarchy of the genres", this was what
governed painting in the XVII century, what
defined the nobility or mundane nature of a
subject, what commanded an artist to become
a historian, moralist, rhetorician, pedagogue
and poet. His paintings would above all aim to
elevate the spirit and draw from the Bible,
history or mythology. As far as landscape, the
portrait, the character scene and still life were
concerned, these were inferior fields. Within
this classification, Lorrain created a new form
of landscape art through the idealized recrea-
tion of Nature, combined with the representation of episodes from antiquity and a
rendering of atmospheric effects.

These works are located in the Sully area,
on the 2nd floor, in rooms 31 and 34

French paintings

Charles Le Brun, *Chancellor Séguier,* c.1655-1657.
Oil on canvas, 295 x 351 cm
Hyacinthe Rigaud, *Louis XIV, king of France,* 1701.
Oil on canvas, 277 x 194 cm

The king and his artists

Amid an unfurling of draperies, ermines, embroidery and lace comes Louis XIV who, for over seventy years, orchestrated artistic life at the court of Versailles. Le Vau, Hardouin-Mansart, Robert de Cotte were involved with architecture, Le Nôtre with the gardens. Le Brun was involved with painting, enjoying the patronage of the Chancellor of France, Séguier, the second most important person in the State - not forgetting Coypel, Mignard or Rigaud. Girardon and Coysevox were involved with sculpture, Bossuet with oratory, Boileau with poetry. Molière, Corneille and Racine were involved with the theatre, Lully, Charpentier, Couperin, Marais with music...

These works are located in the Sully area,
on the 2nd floor, in rooms 36 and 38

French paintings

Jean Antoine Watteau, *Gilles*, c.1718-1720. Oil on canvas, 184 x 149 cm
Jean Antoine Watteau, *Pilgrimage to the Isle of Cythera*, 1717. Oil on canvas,
129 x 194 cm

A soul enamoured of colour

Watteau was one of the favourite painters of
Marcel Proust, who marvelled "to see him build
up through purchases or gifts a real collection of
all the clothes of the Commedia dell'Arte; his
chief pleasure was, when friends came to see him,
to have them dress up in these. Then he begged
them to pose, consoling himself with seeing living
people in such fine unreal costumes, smiling,
bubbly and chatty, carrying within him, always in
an otherwordly state, a soul enamoured of light
and colour. When his friends left, he would stow
away the drawing he had begun and later
incorporate it into a grand composition."

These works are located in the Sully area,
on the 2nd floor, in room 40

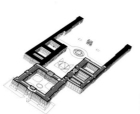

French paintings

Jean-Baptiste Siméon Chardin, *Self-portrait with spectacles*, 1771
Pastel on blue-grey paper, 45.9 x 37.5 cm
Jean-Baptiste Siméon Chardin, *Pipe and drinking-jug*, or *The Smoking-den*,
c.1737. Oil on canvas, 32 x 42 cm
Jean-Baptiste Siméon Chardin, *Saying Grace*, 1740. Oil on canvas, 49.5 x 38.5 cm

Domestic life

In devoting himself to portraying daily life, to his domestic surroundings, Chardin chose to give equal
importance to characters and objects. And whilst the term "still life" is then needed to describe some of
his compositions, it replaces without subtlety expressions more attuned to the notion of a silent life, such
as "restful nature" or "quiet life". It was not so in times past and in other countries: the Italy of the Renaissance
spoke of cose naturali, those "things of nature", Spain evoked "flowers and kitchen nooks", the North
created *still-leven, Stilleben*, "nature unstirring" and captured through the painting.

These works are located in the Sully area,
on the 2nd floor, in room 48

French paintings

François Boucher, *Diana Leaving her Bath*, 1742. Oil on canvas, 56 x 73 cm
Jean Honoré Fragonard, *The Bathers*, c.1772-1775. Oil on canvas, 64 x 80 cm

Towards unbridled gaiety

Fragonard shone in a career pursued away from official circuits, despising royal commands, and
the honours of the Academy and Drawing-rooms [Salons], painting thanks to the support of
collectors and patrons. While his master, Boucher, the favourite artist of Madame de Pompadour,
brought fame to court art under Louis XV through his compositions of naked mythological
figures which adorned studies and sitting-rooms, Fragonard let sensuality drip from his paintings. No quivers, hunting trophies or draperies: in unbridled gaiety, he whips up his bathers
with clear, broad strokes, intertwines the drips from his brush into his colours; and whilst, from
afar, one can discern reeds and foliage, close up, it's a different matter altogether.

These works are located in the Sully area,
on the 2nd floor, in room 48

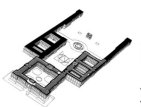

French paintings

Jean Honoré Fragonard, *The Bolt,* c. 1778. Oil on canvas, 73 x 93 cm
Jean Honoré Fragonard, *Inspiration,* 1769. Oil on canvas, 80 x 65 cm
Jean Honoré Fragonard, *Psyche and Eros.* Wash tint, 32 x 45 cm

The staged seduction

In order to describe his art, lovers of Fragonard speak of virtuosity and freedom of brushstroke, dynamism and boldness of composition, whether in his figures of fantasy or in his staging of seduction, banter and love. Thus the painter has no hesitation in placing at the centre of an almost bolted bedroom the immense disorder of a bed created from dishevelled sheets, and movement of forms and colours. Others are less enthusiastic, such as the critic who, hiding behind the name of "Monsieur Tartouillis" ["Mr. Dauber"] in 1773, saw in it nothing but "the ultimate in colours clashing, rolled together, slapped about, daubed on".

These works are is located in the Sully area,
on the 2nd floor, in room 51

French paintings

Jean-Baptiste Greuze, *The Village Bride*, 1761,
Oil on canvas, 92 x 117 cm
Jean-Baptiste Greuze, *The Broken Pitcher*, 1772-1773.
Oil on canvas, 108.5 x 86.5 cm

"Moralize in your paintings"

Greuze passionately dreamed only of one thing: to attain the noble title of painter of history, to belong to the lineage of the great Nicolas Pousssin. But all his success came from these rustic scenes, in which he exalts with a great many pathetic gestures and tearful effects the traditional virtues of the peasant family: filial piety, the authority of the father, marriage. The greatly vexed artist nevertheless found in Diderot one of the most fervent of admirers: "Take heart, Greuze my friend, moralize in your paintings, and always carry on like that."

These works are located in the Denon wing, on the 1st floor, in room 75

French paintings

Jacques Louis David, *The Coronation of Napoleon I, 2nd December 1804,* 1806-1807. Oil on canvas, 621 x 979 cm
Jacques Louis David, *The Sabine Women,* 1799. Oil on canvas, 385 x 522 cm
Detail double page overleaf

Antiquity and the Empire

The history of the Sabine women is a history of family: in order to ensure descendants for their newly-emerging country, the Romans carried off the women of the Sabine people. Three years passed. Determined to avenge themselves, the vanquished returned to the place of the abduction. Then the women entered into the battle and placed themselves between those who had become their husbands and those who were their fathers and brothers. This is the moment chosen by David, the Jacobin of the revolutionary years, and the leader of neo-classicism. In showing his work in 1799, he defended the decision he had made: to show his heroes naked. "My intention, in creating this picture, was to paint the ancient practices with such accuracy that the Greeks and Romans, in seeing my work, would not have found me alien to their customs." A few years later, David turned to current events: he placed himself in the service of the empire, somewhat overlooking his position of former times.

This work is located in the Denon wing, on the 1st floor, in room 77

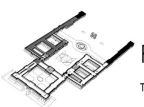

French paintings

Théodore Géricault, *The Raft of the Medusa*, 1819. Oil on canvas, 491 x 716 cm

Violation of painting

"Where does it come from? I do not know that touch", complained David, the former neo-classical master. "Where is its centre?", panicked a critic. "It only has one fault, it's that he has forgotten to paint it", noted a shrewd observer... If Géricault was covered with insults and caused a scandal, it is that he dared elevate an incident to the dimensions reserved for the painting of history, and that was by the violence of his contrasts, his thick brownish paint and the greenish tonality of his bodies.

These works are located in the Denon wing,
on the 1st floor, in room 77

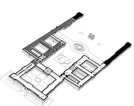

French paintings

Eugène Delacroix, *The Death of Sardanapalus*, 1827. Oil on canvas, 392 x 496 cm
Eugène Delacroix, *The Women of Algiers*, 1834. Oil on canvas, 180 x 229 cm

Romantic colour

"Painters who are not colourists do illumination and not painting. Painting as such, unless one wishes to execute a colourless composition, incorporates the idea of colour as one of the necessary bases, as much as light-dark, proportion and perspective. Proportion applies to sculpture as to painting; perspective determines the outline; light-dark causes features to stand out through the arrangement of light and shade in relation to the background; colour gives the semblance of life"

Eugène Delacroix, *Journal*,
23rd February 1852.

This work is located in the Denon wing, on the 1st floor, in room 77

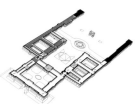

French paintings

Eugène Delacroix, *The 28th of July 1830: Liberty Guiding the People*, 1830. Oil on canvas, 260 x 325 cm

Liberty guides Delacroix

"When I met Delacroix on the 27th July beside the Arcole bridge and he pointed out to me some of those men one only sees at times of revolution, and who were sharpening on the cobblestones, one a sabre, the other a foil, Delacroix revealed his fear to me in the most emphatic manner. But when Delacroix saw the tricolour floating over Notre Dame [...], ah! upon my word, his manner changed, enthusiasm replaced fear, and he glorified these people who, earlier, had frightened him", recalls Alexandre Dumas. A few months later, the painter devoted a huge canvas to the "Three Glorious Days" those dates in 1830 during which Parisians deposed Charles X.

These works are located in the Denon wing,
on the 1st floor, in room 75

French paintings

Jean Auguste Dominique Ingres, *La Grande Odalisque,* 1814.
Oil on canvas, 91 x 162 cm
Théodore Chassériau, *Esther at her Ablutions,* 1841. Oil on canvas, 45.5 x 35.5 cm

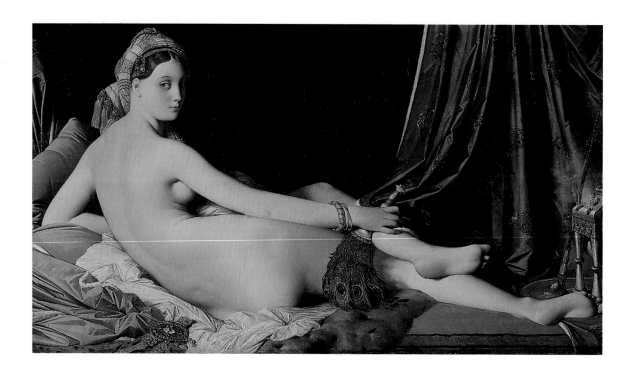

A line to be followed

Drawing or colour? What should be given priority? That was the quarrel that caused painters to clash during the XIX century. Ingres, an omnipotent master at the École des Beaux Arts [Academy of Fine Arts], adhered with the utmost steadfastness to the former: drawing is the probity of art, it "forms three-quarters and a half of the painting. If I had to put a sign above my door, I would write: *School of Drawing,* and I am sure I would make painters". For "beautiful forms are straight outlines with rounded lines. Beautiful forms are those which are firm and full. The form must have a good constitution". A line which his pupil, Chassériau, did not follow, from then on incurring the master's disapproval: he is nothing but an insubordinate, a traitor who has defected to the colour camp.

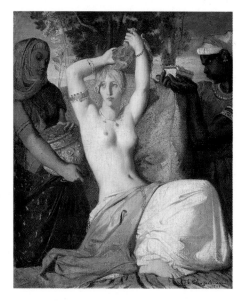

These works are located in the Sully area,
on the 2nd floor, in room 60

French paintings

Jean Auguste Dominique Ingres, *The Valpinçon Bather,* 1808.
Oil on canvas, 146 x 97 cm
Jean Auguste Dominique Ingres, *The Turkish Bath,* 1862. Oil on canvas,
diameter: 110 cm

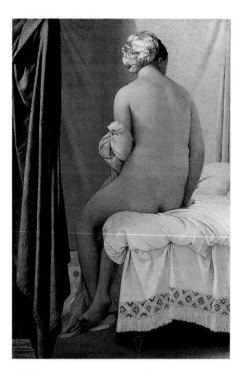

Women at the bath

Ingres was eighty-two years old when he finished his painting: the sum of half a century's study of the female body, starting
with *The Valpinçon Bather.* No doubt he was so glad to have come to the end of it that he added his age beside his
signature. It is a true spectacle of damp curves, languid softness, voluptuous flesh and limbs stretched out as if more
fully to mould around the circular format of the picture. This view of a harem found no favour with the Emperess Eugénie,
nauseated by such an accumulation of Eastern nudes, nor with Baudelaire, unable to bear the anatomical distortions:
"Here we'll find a navel straying towards the ribs, there a breast pointing too far towards the armpit; here we are
completely disconcerted by an unspeakable leg."

These works are located in the Sully area,
on the 2nd floor, in room 73

French paintings

Camille Corot, *Souvenir of Mortefontaine,* 1864. Oil on canvas, 65 x 89 cm
Camille Corot, *Tivoli. The Gardens of the Villa d'Este,* 1843. Oil on canvas,
43.5 x 60.5 cm
Camille Corot, *Woman in Blue,* 1874. Oil on canvas, 80 x 50.5 cm

In memory of nature

"If M. Corot were to consent to do away, once and for all, with the
nymphs with which he populates his woods, and to replace them with
countrywomen, I would appreciate him beyond measure", declared
Émile Zola in 1866. Clearly, the writer never met the painter. Whether
or not he places poetic figures in his compositions is doubtless not the
most important issue: Corot was before all else sensitive to the changing
effects of light, reflections on water, the fluidity of the air. A sensitivity
which young artists such as Sisley or Monet would soon recognize in
themselves; those artists who would be called the Impressionists would
show their admiration for the representation of nature as for the portraits
of their elder.

These works are located in the Denon wing, on the 1st floor, in room 3

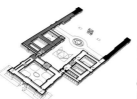

Italian paintings

Cenni di Pepi, known as Cimabue, *The Virgin and Child in Majesty surrounded by Six Angels,* c.1270. Tempera on wood, 427 x 280 cm
Giotto di Bondone, *St. Francis of Assisi Receiving the Stigmata,* c.1295-1300. Tempera on wood, 313 x 163 cm

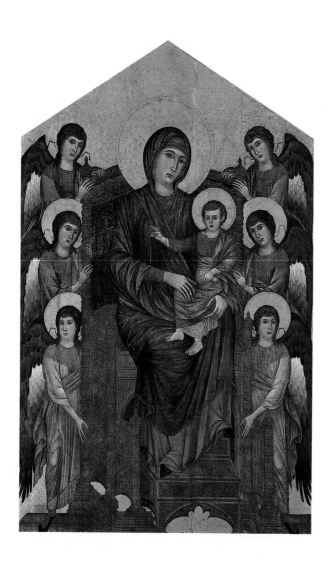

Master and pupil

According to tradition, Cimabue discovered the young Giotto who was drawing his flock of sheep, and then decided to train him in his Florentine studio. A new century began between the time of the painting by the master and that of the pupil, a century which would be marked by a development in the style of painting: the XIV century, the Italian Trecento, was on its way. Whilst Cimabue was portraying a *Maestà* [Majesty], a dignified Virgin standing out against a gold background, according to the rules of Byzantine tradition, Giotto was paying homage to the saint of the poor by attending to the relief, to nature and space: a mountain in perspective, trees with distinct foliage, birds of different kinds.

This work is located in the Denon wing,
on the 1st floor, in room 3

Italian paintings

Guido di Pietro, known as Fra Angelico, *The Coronation of the Virgin,*
c.1430-1435. Tempera on wood, 209 x 206 cm

Retable for the virgin

Working for the monastery of San Domenico of Fiesole, Fra Angelico devoted the upper level
of his retable to the Virgin, but reserved the predella - the lower part - for certain episodes
from the saint's legend. Thus, Dominic wrote a work against the heretics and gave it to one of
them to prove to him the omnipotence of his religion. Surrounded by a number of friends, the
man submitted it to the ordeal by fire. He made three attempts, but nothing happened to it:
this strange work did not burn... The greatly vexed heretic wanted to keep what had occurred
a secret, but a soldier had witnessed it and went off to recount it. Such was the miracle of
the book.

These works are located in the Denon wing, on the 1st floor, in room 4

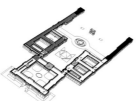

Italian paintings

Piero della Francesca, *Portrait of Sigismond Malatesta,* c.1451.
Oil on wood, 44 x 34 cm
Antonello da Messina, *Portrait of a Man, or The Condottiere,* 1475.
Oil on wood, 36.2 x 30 cm
Antonio Pisano, known as Pisanello, *Portrait of a Princess of Este,* c.1436-1438.
Oil on wood, 43 x 30 cm

Courtiers and travellers

The painters of the Quattrocento were itinerant painters: they went from court to court, placing themselves in the service of princes, painting to order. Thus, based in Ferrara, Pisanello shows a princess from the Este family against a background of carnations and butterflies. Faced with Sigismond Malatesta, lord of Rimini, Piero della Francesca paints a portrait of the strictest geometrical construction. As for Antonello da Messina, he resided for a while in Venice, where he painted Sforza Maria Sforza, duke of Bari. In this way does the history of the Italian Renaissance take shape from one city to another.

These works are located in the Denon wing,
on the 1st floor, in room 3

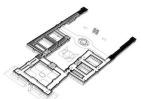

Italian paintings

Paolo Uccello, *The Battle of San Romano,* c.1455-1456. Tempera on wood, 182 x 317 cm
Antonio Pisano, known as Pisanello, *Two Horses,* first half of the XV century. Pen, ink and black chalk. 20 x 16.6 cm

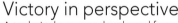

Victory in perspective

A technical process developed from the XV century onwards would enable painters to give the illusion of space, to produce depth: to these new processes afforded by perspective, Uccello abandoned himself with fervour, whether it be linear - all lines converging on a single vanishing point -, or aerial - based on the gradation and alternating of shades. The victory won by the Florentine *condottiere* Micheletto da Cotignola over the Siennese is the pretext for a display of brilliance.

This work is located in the Denon wing,
on the 1st floor, in room 5

Italian paintings

Andrea Mantegna, *St Sebastian*, c.1480. Tempera on wood, 255 x 140 cm

A passion for Antiquity

How to demonstrate his passion for Antiquity, prove his mastery of
perspective and ultimately, pay homage to a Christian martyr? Mantegna
took up this challenge and delivered a proclamation of the humanist
culture to his patrons, the Gonzaga family of Mantua. He studied,
invented, recomposed: a portico in ruins with volutes and acanthi,
architectural remains, a sculptured foot, a town in the background
which blends contemporary and ancient buildings, and even the body
of the saint, pierced with arrows, whose bust is painted in the style of
a statue from antiquity.

These works are located in the Denon wing,
on the 1st floor, in room 2

Italian paintings

Sandro di Mariano Filipepi, known as Botticelli, *Venus and the Graces offering Gifts to a Young Woman,* c.1480-1483. Fresco, 211 x 283 cm
Domenico Ghirlandaio, *Portrait of an Old Man and Little Boy,* c.1488. Tempera on wood, 63 x 46 cm

A sophisticated charm

"Whoever does not have an equal liking for everything that pertains to painting is not universal. If, for example, he is not drawn by the landscape, he will say that it is a simple thing and easy to understand; thus our Botticelli said that it was a vain study for it sufficed to throw a sponge soaked with various colours at a wall for it to leave a mark wherein one can perceive a beautiful landscape"... That was the judgement borne by Leonardo da Vinci in respect of the man who, insensitive to nature, charmed his contemporaries with his "sophistication". As for Ghirlandaio, he was highly appreciated for his portraits of the Florentine upper middle class.

These works are located in the Denon wing,
on the 1st floor, in room 5

Italian paintings

Leonardo da Vinci, *The Virgin of the Rocks,* 1483-1486. Oil on canvas,
199 x 122 cm
Leonardo da Vinci, *The Virgin, the Infant Jesus and St Anne,* (detail), c.1508-1510.
Oil on wood, 168 x 130 cm
Leonardo da Vinci, *Head of a Young Woman* c. 1480-1485. Silver point and white
highlights 18 x 16.8 cm
Leonardo da Vinci, *Portrait of a Lady of the Court of Milan,* or *La Belle
Ferronnière,* 1490-1495. Oil on wood, 63 x 45 cm

Power of light and shade

"If you wish to see whether the overall effect of your painting corresponds to the object represented according to nature, take a mirror and place it so as to reflect the real object, then
compare the reflection with your painting and carefully consider whether the subject of both
images conforms to both [...]. Mirror and painting show the images of things bathed in light and
shade. Both one and the other seem to extend considerably away from the plane of their surface. And as you know that the mirror shows you objects clearly thanks to the contours, dark
and light, and that in addition you have at your disposal colours of dark and light more powerful that it has, it is certain that your painting, if you know how to compose it properly, will
likewise show the effect of something natural seen in a large mirror."

Leonardo da Vinci, *Treatise on Painting.*

This work is located in the Denon wing,
on the 1st floor, in room 6

Italian paintings

Leonardo da Vinci, *Portrait of Lisa Gherardini del Giocondo,* known as *La Gioconda* or *Monna Lisa,* c.1503-1506. Oil on wood, 77 x 53 cm

A smile, a landscape

Everyone, painters, writers or theoreticians, has been fascinated by the skill of Leonardo, the Florentine master of sfumato: the man who painted the fluidity and humidity of the air, who portrayed the subtlety of atmospheric effects, allowed light to slide into shade and blurred the outlines of objects or bodies in order to merge them more effectively with the surrounding landscape. Whether it was in the portrait of a young woman in mourning with veiled black hair, the famous Mona Lisa or to drape huge figures against a misty background.

These works are located in the Denon wing, on the 1st floor, in rooms 5 and 6

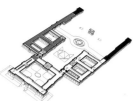

Italian paintings

Raffaello Sanzio, known as Raphael, *The Virgin, Child and little St John,* or *La Belle Jardinière,* 1508. Oil on wood, 122 x 80 cm
Raffaello Sanzio, known as Raphael, *Raphael and a Friend,* 1519. Oil on canvas, 99 x 83 cm
Raffaello Sanzio, known as Raphael, *Portrait of Baldassare Castiglione,* 1514-1515. Oil on canvas, 82 x 67 cm

Announcement of the Passion

Everything appears calm. The Virgin, looking almost like a countrywoman and almost like a "refined tenderer of the garden" ["jardinière"], is seated on a rock, her face standing out against the sky and framed by clouds. The landscape is of the simplest kind, a meadow dotted with a few flowers, spindly trees, hills, a village in the distance. But everything is woven around the poses and the expressions. Raising his eyes towards his mother and leaning on her, the Child tries to grasp the book - in which is told the time of the sacrifice. Kneeling, St John is facing Jesus and is about to stand up again - to give him the cross. Amid a scene of utter serenity we glimpse the announcement of the Passion of Christ.

The humanist ideal

In painting the portrait of Baldassare Castiglione, Raphael illustrates the precepts advocated by that erudite and extremely well-read diplomat, author of *The Courtier* and exalter of the humanist ideal of the XVI century. Art was to disguise all effort, all study and to adorn lines with restraint. What was called elegance: a simple pose, discreet harmony of shades and materials, a light stroke which here and there catches the light or glances off a delicate canvas. All this, Raphael gives us: his face with the light shining straight on it, Castiglione is placed at the level of the observer; similarly, in the painter's self-portrait, a man is pointing at something or someone with his hand.

This work is located in the Denon wing, on the 1st floor, in room 6

Italian paintings

Tiziano Vecellio, known as Titien (attributed to), *The Country Concert,* c.1510.
Oil on canvas, 105 x 137 cm

A venetian paradise

A Venetian nobleman is playing the lute, a countryman is leaning towards him; a woman is pouring water, another holds a flute; in the distance, a shepherd guides his flock. Is this a simple pastoral scene? A vision of Arcady, that place on high of joy and innocence for the ancient writers? Could it be an allegory - the lute symbolizes lyric poetry -, a musical joust between the townsman's stringed instrument and the rustic wind instrument? Do the women represent the Muses? Such a painting is the reflection of the culture of a man of the Renaissance, the scope of which nowadays we have difficulty attaining.

These works are located in the Denon wing, on the 1st floor, in room 6

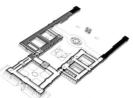

Italian paintings

Paolo Caliari, known as **Veronese**, *The Wedding Feast at Cana*, 1562-1563. Oil on canvas, 677 x 994 cm. *Detail double page overleaf*
Antonio Allegri, known as **Correggio**, *The Mystic Marriage of St Catherine of Alexandria*, c.1526-1527. Oil on wood, 105 x 102 cm
In Parma, Correggio developed an original colouring based on golden harmonies and warm velvety tones.

Piety and music

"There was a wedding feast at Cana in Galilee, and the mother of Jesus was there. Jesus was also invited to the wedding feast, and his disciples. Now there was no more wine." So Jesus turned the water into wine and thus performed the first miracle. Using this passage from the Gospel according to St John, Veronese displays his skill with space and his chromatic brilliance to embellish the refectory of the Venetian abbey of San Giorgio Maggiore. To reproaches of having yielded to exaggeration and luxuriance to the detriment of the biblical scene, Veronese called upon artistic licence: "We, as painters, we take the same liberty as poets and madmen." It is in the name of that liberty that he chose to paint Jesus at the centre of a crowd of contemporary characters dressed in the Venetian or Turkish style, to include jesters and dogs, all details considered unseemly, and to place a group of musicians in the foreground: the man in red is playing the double bass viol, to his right another is holding a kit; the man in white and the one sitting behind him are on the viola; in the background, one is blowing a cornet whilst the man in the turban, to the left, is playing the sackbut.

These works are located in the Denon wing,
on the 1st floor, in room 7

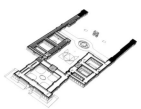

Italian paintings

Michelangelo Merisi, known as Caravaggio, *The Fortune-teller*, c.1594.
Oil on canvas, 99 x 131 cm
Michelangelo Merisi, known as Caravaggio, *The Death of the Virgin*, 1605-1606.
Oil on canvas, 369 x 245 cm

Slices of life

A woman of humble origins has just died; only a delicate halo identifies her as the Virgin. A gipsy girl outwits a nobleman and steals his ring. In order to portray his characters, Caravaggio sought his models in the street. This is what the historian Bellori recounts: "Scorning the most famous marble statues of Antiquity and the so celebrated paintings of Raphael, he offered nature alone as the subject for his brush; he held out his hand to the crowd to show that nature had endowed it well enough with masters". This fine lesson in naturalism would not forgotten by those painters of the XVII century known as the "Caravagists".

These works are located in the Denon wing, on the 1st floor, in rooms 7

Italian paintings

Francesco Guardi, *The Doge of Venice on his way to the church of La Salute on 21st November, the day of the commemoration of the plague of 1630,* c.1766-1770. Oil on canvas, 67 x 100 cm
Francesco Guardi, *Venice, San Giorgio Maggiore,* c.1766-1770. Oil on canvas, 67 x 100 cm
Giandomenico Tiepolo, *Carnival Scene,* c.1754-1755. Oil on canvas, 80 x 110 cm

The doge and the carnival

Very many are the lovers of Venice and its carnival; very many were those who, in the XVIII century, were drawn by the festivities offered by the Venetian Republic, whether they were artists or dilettantes. "The carnival begins on the 5th of October", wrote Charles de Brosses, an itinerant writer, "and there is another small one lasting a fortnight at Ascension; so that here one can allow around six months during which everyone goes around in a mask, whether priest or anyone else, even the nuncio and the Superior of the Capuchins."

This work is located in the Richelieu wing,
on the 2nd floor, in room 4

Flemish paintings

Jan van Eyck, *The Virgin at the home of Chancellor Rolin,* c.1435.
Oil on wood, 66 x 62 cm

The donor's chapel

In painting four scenes, in structuring his work on several levels, Van Eyck draws our gaze,
leading it around gradually in order more effectively to give us the illusion of depth and the immen-
sity of the painted area. The donor is praying to the Virgin in a room with a tiled floor, then a
garden is shown, then comes a terrace which overhangs a river winding through an urban
landscape as far as the mountains. But today another scene is missing, the one for which the
work was designed: the Rolin family chapel in the cathedral of Autun. It is evoked in the painting:
in order to balance the distribution of light, the artist from Bruges has illuminated the characters
from the right, taking into account where the picture would hang in the chapel, lit from the left.

These works are located in the Richelieu wing,
on the 2nd floor, in room 4

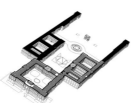

Flemish paintings

Rogier van der Weyden, *The Annunciation,* c.1435. Oil on wood, 86 x 93 cm
Rogier van der Weyden, *The Braque Family Triptych:* Christ between the Virgin
and St John the Evangelist, St John the Baptist (left) and St Madeleine (right),
c.1450-1452. Oil on wood, 41 x 68 cm (centre panel), 41 x 35 cm (wings)

Private devotion

The retable was originally a *tabula de retro,* a "board placed behind" the altar table in a church on which
were lain the objects of worship. This original use was soon replaced by another, decorative and symbo-
lic: sculptured or painted, the retable, by its images, indicates the presence of God or patron saints.
Increasingly complicated, it was divided into panels and surmounted by a canopy or by a 'heaven above'.
Then it was used as a medium for private devotion and became portable; made up of two, three or a
number of volets, it became a diptych, triptych or polyptych. Its owner would have his portrait or coat of
arms painted on the back of the volets, and carried it with him wherever his travels took him. Piety was also
practised at home.

These works are located in the Richelieu wing, on the 2nd floor, in room 5

Flemish paintings

Hans Memling, *Triptych of Resurrection,* the martyr St Sebastian (left) and the Ascension (right), c.1490. Oil on wood, 61 x 44 cm (centre panel), 61 x 18 cm (wings)
Hans Memling, *Angel holding an Olive Branch,* Oil on wood, 16.4 x 11 cm

A Primitive ?

"Go to the Museum one Sunday, you'll find, at a certain point in the gallery, your way blocked by a crowd gathered around a picture, and it's the same every Sunday. You think its a masterpiece; not at all: it's a daub from the German school." This is how Stendhal expressed all the admiration he felt before a triptych by Memling so admired by the public at the Louvre in 1814. Today considered as one of the great representatives of the Northern school, this painter of Germanic origin who settled in Bruges was formerly classified under the title of "Primitive", not belonging to the "Renaissance", judged as the mature period of painting. The history of tastes is a fluctuating one.

This work is located in the Richelieu wing, on the 2nd floor, in room 9

Flemish paintings

Quentin Metsys, *The Moneylender and his Wife,* 1514. Oil on wood, 70 x 67 cm

The painter and his mirror

Whereas the objects lying around the studio are shown here to depict the profession of the usurer - rings, pearls, coins, a balance, books and parchments -, a number of details are there to suggest other places and to open upon other spaces: to the right, a door is ajar; to the left, a reflection strikes light off the belly of a bottle; in the centre, the image of a man reading near a window, beyond which is a landscape, is shown in a mirror. A convex mirror, one of the kind known as "witches" in the Middle Ages since, due to their irregular surface, they distort the face of the person looking into them. An allegory for sight, perception and reflection, the mirror is also the emblem of the artist who enjoys showing one reality whilst reflecting another, who plays with the seen and the unseen, what is in the frame and out-of-range. The mirror is the painter's allusion.

These works are located in the Richelieu wing, on the 2nd floor, in room 18

Flemish paintings

Peter Paul Rubens, *The Queen's Arrival at Marseilles, on the 3rd November 1600,* ninth painting in the cycle devoted to Maria de' Medici, 1622-1625.
Oil on canvas, 394 x 295 cm
Peter Paul Rubens, *The Fair,* c.1635. Oil on wood, 149 x 261 cm
Antoon van Dyck (after), *Portrait of Rubens and Van Dyck,* copy from the XIX century. Oil on canvas, 58 x 74 cm

The grace of curves

How to paint a woman? In his *Theory of the Human Form, studied from its principles, either at rest or in motion,* the Flemish master stated a model of beauty. Whereas the body of a man is defined by the cube and the square, that of a woman is governed by the circle. With women, rounded forms and curves predominate: the unwrinkled face with the plump neck, the rather soft arms, the long hand with nimble fingers, the ample chest with a touch of elevation, the skin around the belly with gentle, flowing contours, the right leg from which the full flesh elegantly protrudes, the wide, plump thighs, the rolled buttocks, the tiny foot. The whole body white of flesh and tinged with pale red.

This work is located in the Richelieu wing, on the 2nd floor, in room 5

Dutch paintings

Hieronymus Bosch, *The Ship of Fools,* c.1490-1500. Oil on wood, 58 x 32 cm

The drunken boat

What is this strange, frail hull in which a jester, a nun, a Franciscan monk and other characters drink, vomit, and attempt, mouths agape, to catch hold of some sort of cake or to get at a chicken tied to the mast? Where are they drifting to? Dear to the Flemish tradition, the boatful of revellers appears in popular literature, in carnival processions and songs, vilifying the folly of all those who, corrupted and debauched, have turned away from Christian values and are sailing towards Hell.

These works are located in the Richelieu wing,
on the 2nd floor, in room 30

Dutch paintings

Gerard ter Borch, *The Duet: Singer and Theorbo Player*, 1669. Oil on canvas.
82.5 x 72 cm
Frans Hals, *The Jester on the Lute*, c.1624. Oil on canvas, 70 x 62 cm
Frans Hals, *The Bohemian Girl*, c.1628-1630. Oil on canvas, 58 x 52 cm

Playing the lute

There is between a figure of fantasy painted by Frans Hals and a society genre scene refined by Ter Borch doubtless nothing in common in terms of pictorial practice. On the other hand, what does connect this jester and the duet of musicians is the symbol par excellence for music, the most valued stringed instrument of the XVII century, one which enjoyed the highest esteem: the lute. Played as an accompaniment to the voice or on its own, the simple lute or the theorbo - one of its variants -, is "the noblest of all, by virtue of the sweetness of its songs, the number and harmony of its chords, its range, its melodiousness, and the difficulty it presents in playing it", wrote Marin Mersenne in 1636 in his *Universal Harmony*.

These works are located in the Richelieu wing,
on the 2nd floor, in room 31

Dutch paintings

Rembrandt Harmensz. van Rijn, *Portrait of the Artist at his Easel,* 1660.
Oil on canvas, 111 x 90 cm
Rembrandt Harmensz. van Rijn, *Bathsheba Bathing,* 1654.
Oil on canvas, 142 x 142 cm
Rembrandt Harmensz. Van Rijn, *Rembrandt Pouting.* 1630. Etching, 7.5 x 7.5 cm

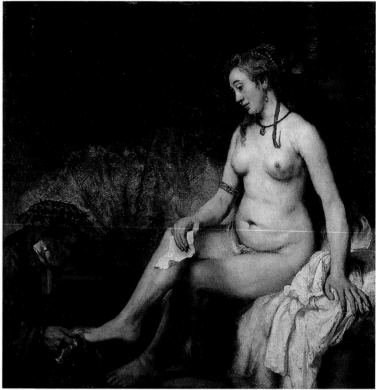

The concubine-servant

"It happened that, towards evening, David, having got up from his couch and strolling on the roof of the palace, saw from there a woman bathing. The woman was very beautiful. David sent to find out who she was, and the answer came:" She is Bathsheba, daughter of Eliam and wife of Uriah the Hittite!" Then David sent messengers to fetch her. She came to him and he had intercourse with her, though she had just been purified after menstruation." Whilst he chose to paint a very well-known biblical episode, Rembrandt Harmenszoon, son of the miller Harmen van Rijn, concentrated on the nude - the model for which was his servant and concubine Hendrickje Stoffels -, dispensing with any anecdotal details.

This work is located in the Richelieu wing,
on the 2nd floor, in room 38

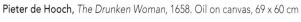

Dutch paintings

Pieter de Hooch, *The Drunken Woman*, 1658. Oil on canvas, 69 x 60 cm

The picture within a picture

To paint an interior with its succession of rooms and its breaks where the light shines through, then to bring together men and their lady friends around a glass of wine: this is how to compose one of the most typical scenes of Dutch genre painting. Hung behind the characters, canvases complete the setting - such as the map of Amsterdam against which a young man is framed - but they also add a moralizing touch to the whole scene: do we not recognize on the right a representation of Christ and the adulteress ? Pieter de Hooch liked to tell stories in his pictures and in the pictures in his picture.

These works are located in the Richelieu wing,
on the 2nd floor, in room 38

Dutch paintings

Johannes Vermeer, *The Lacemaker,* c.1670-1671.
Oil on canvas mounted on wood, 24 x 21 cm
Johannes Vermeer, *The Astronomer,* 1668. Oil on canvas, 51 x 45 cm

Enclosed and silent life

Wermeer did not live off his painting: a fairly fortunate family, a patron buying canvases from him and lending him money, his business as an art dealer finally enabled him to restrict his production to two or three works a year and to have complete freedom to choose his subjects, whether it be scenes of domesticity or study. Such was not the situation for most Dutch artists who sold their pictures at fairs, at public buildings or from their studio, pictures which were valued according to their size, theme and the manner in which it was painted: thus a painting with figures was more expensive than a still life or landscape since it required more time and effort.

This work is located in the Richelieu wing, on the 2nd floor, in room 8

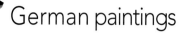

German paintings

Albrecht Dürer, *Portrait of the Artist holding a Thistle,* 1493. Oil on parchment mounted on canvas, 56.5 x 44.5 cm
Albrecht Dürer, *The Arco Valley,* 1495. Watercolour and gouache with overstrokes using pen and black ink, 22.3 x 22.2 cm

The art of measurement

The art of measurement being the foundation for all painting, wrote Dürer, "I proposed to give the elements thereof and to explain its principles to young people wishing to educate themselves in their art, so that they may confidently start measuring with a pair of compasses and ruler, thereby recognizing and having before their eyes the genuine truth, so that they have not only the wish to acquaint themselves with the arts but that they may also attain a true and deeper understanding of them; and in that I did not take into account the fact that some people, in our country and our times, hold the art of painting in profound contempt". We are in Nuremberg at the start of the XVI century.

These works are located in the Richelieu wing,
on the 2nd floor, in room 8

German paintings

Lucas Cranach, The Elder, *Portrait assumed to be Magdalena Luther,* daughter of Martin Luther, c.1540. Oil on wood, 39 x 25 cm
Lucas Cranach, The Elder, *Venus,* 1529. Oil on wood, 33 x 26 cm

Cranach's studio

Nearly four hundred works emerged from the studio of Lucas, a native of Cranach. Four hundred works which reflect the activity of the man who, for fifty years, placed himself in service to the court of the Electors of Saxony at Wittenberg. Works which were also the result of commissions from many private clients. Thus were produced religious paintings or mythological scenes, figures of Venus naked against a landscape or portraits of distinguished people, young girls and friends, such as Martin Luther. It was, moreover, at Wittenberg that the Reformation began: it was here in 1517 that the theologian nailed up ninety-five theses which earned him excommunication, and it was here too that he burned the papal bull ordering him to recant.

These works are located in the Richelieu wing,
on the 2nd floor, in room 8

German paintings

Hans Holbein, The Younger, *Erasmus*, 1523. Oil on wood, 42 x 32 cm
Hans Holbein, The Younger, *Nikolas Kratzer*, 1528. Oil on wood, 83 x 67 cm

Write, observe, calculate

One is writing, the other is observing and calculating. The
former is a Dutch theologian, author of *Colloquia* and the
Praise of Folly, the latter is a German astronomer settled in
London. In painting Erasmus and Nikolas Kratzer at work
- surrounded by measuring instruments, compasses, rulers
and a sundial -, in paying tribute to the men of learning of
his time, Hans Holbein became the portrait painter of
humanism in the XVI century.

This work is located in the Denon wing,
on the 1st floor, in room 13

Spanish paintings

Domenikos Theotokopoulos,known as El Greco, *Christ on the Cross adored by Two Donors,* c.1580. Oil on canvas, 250 x 180 cm

The greek from Toledo

"Who would have thought that Domenico Greco often went over his paintings, and used to retouch them, to leave the colours clear and distinct and to give them that appearance of cruel blemishes, like a pretence of vigour", wondered the painter Francisco Pacheco, who met El Greco in Toledo. "I was very surprised when I asked Domenico Greco in 1611 which was the most difficult, drawing or colour - he replied: "colour." And what is even more astonishing was to hear him talk with such little respect for Michelangelo - the Father of painting -, saying that he was a great man, but that he didn't know how to paint".

These works are located in the Denon wing,
on the 1st floor, in room 13

Spanish paintings

Francisco de Zurbaràn, *The Lying-in-State of St Bonaventura,* c.1629.
Oil on canvas, 250 x 225 cm
Bartolomé Esteban Murillo, *The Young Beggar,* c.1650. Oil on canvas,
137 x 115 cm
Jusepe de Ribera, *The Club-footed Boy,* 1642. Oil on canvas, 164 x 92 cm

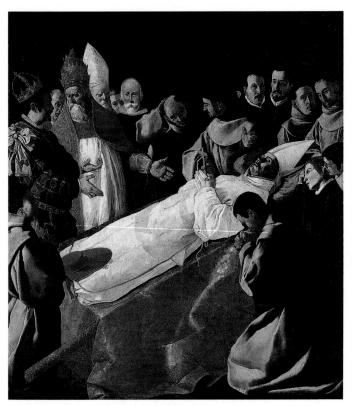

A golden age

If the XVII century is called the Spanish "Golden Age", it is because its paintings
display rare brilliance and abundance. The extremely Catholic kingdom demanded
from artists the expression of an austere piety as well as charitable concern for the
weakest and most deprived in society. In Seville, Zurbarán paid homage to a
Franciscan saint whilst Murillo applied himself to depicting a beggar. In Naples - then
under Spanish rule - Ribera painted a great portrait of a little club-footed boy.

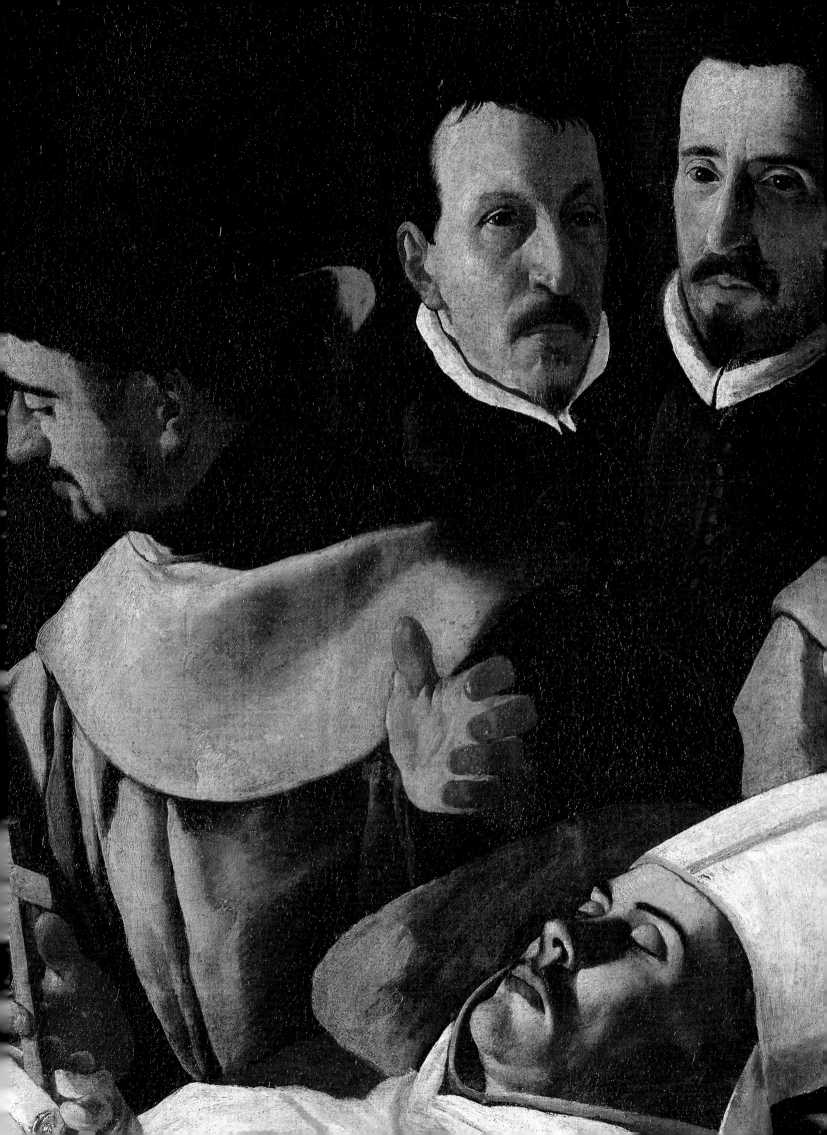

These works are located in the Sully Area,
on the 2nd floor, in room A

Spanish paintings

Francisco de Goya y Lucientes, *Woman with Fan,* 1805-1810. Oil on canvas,
103 x 83 cm
Francisco de Goya y Lucientes, *Portrait of Zurbarán.* Drawing. Sanguine,
15.2 x 11.8 cm
Francisco de Goya y Lucientes, *Portrait of the Condesa del Carpio known* as
La Solana, c.1793-1794. Oil on canvas, 181 x 122 cm

The king's painter

Under his title of *pintor de cámara,* painter of the royal chamber of Charles IV, Goya
has left an impressive collection of portraits of the Madrid Court, and of the
aristocracy and the cultivated society of his time: king and queen, bank director,
general, ambassador, collector or painter - such as Francisco de Zurbarán -, all filed
past him. Not forgetting the ladies of nobility: the Condesa del Carpio, Marquesa
de la Solana, portrayed in a harmony of grey set off by a pink ribbon, or a woman
with a fan.

These works are located in the Sully wing,
on the 1st floor, in room 74

English paintings

Thomas Gainsborough, *Conversation in a Park*, c.1746-1747.
Oil on canvas, 73 x 68 cm
Thomas Gainsborough, *Lady Alston*, c.1760-1765. Oil on canvas, 226 x 168 cm
Joshua Reynolds, *Master Hare*, c.1788-1789. Oil on canvas, 77 x 63 cm

Landscape portraits

"Poetry, Painting and Gardening (or science of the landscape) will always, in the eyes of people of taste, be
the Three Sisters or the Three New Graces that clothe Nature and embellish it", preached the writer Horace
Walpole. Developing new landscape aesthetics, the England of the XVIII century saw picturesque, ran-
domly-growing gardens take shape, some punctuated with poetic allusions, dotted with mock ruins or
exotic summerhouses, others seeking to imitate nature with hills and undergrowth. It was these gardens
that artists chose as a backdrop for their aristocratic portraits.

These works are located in the Denon wing,
on the 1st floor, in room 76

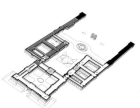

English paintings

John Constable, *View of Salisbury*, c.1820. Oil on canvas, 35 x 51 cm
John Constable, *Panoramic Landscape*. Watercolour. 19.5 x 34.5 cm
Joseph Mallord William Turner, *Landscape with a River and a Bay in the Distance*, c.1840-1845. Oil on canvas, 93 x 123 cm

Sky and water

Whereas Constable rarely left the region of his birth and tirelessly used to paint its countryside, making ever more studies of skies and clouds, Turner travelled throughout England and the Continent. The former wanted, he said, to become a "natural painter", committed to simple, authentic representation; as for the latter, he would carry out quite a different type of research on light, turning his landscapes into whirlpools of colour. And whereas Constable's pictures seemed able to be deciphered by his contemporaries, those of Turner, on the other hand, were judged incomprehensible.

Graphic arts

Jean Fouquet, *Caesar crossing the Rubicon,* page from *Ancient History as far as Caesar and Deeds of the Romans,* c.1470-1475.
Illumination on vellum, 44 x 32.5 cm
Antonio Pisano, known as Pisanello, *Tufted Lapwing, Great Spotted Woodpecker and Partridge,* XV century. Watercolor, white highlights, brown ink, lead points and black chalk, 15.7 x 28.9 cm, 9 x 14.7 cm and 17 x 19.2 cm
Leonardo da Vinci, *Drapery for a Kneeling Figure,* Grey tempera with white highlights on grey canvas, 20.7 x 28.1 cm

Pens and brushes

The roughly one hundred and thirty thousand drawings in the Louvre testify to the diversity of the techniques employed by artists using brush, pen or metal point. The "stone of Italy" or "black stone" [black chalk], is often used with sanguine, highlighted with white chalk; inks are thinned with wash tints; bistre is a brown obtained using soot, water and gum; tempera is egg-based. Canvases and papers are sometimes dyed; vellums are parchments made from the skins of young or stillborn animals, lambs or foals.

Graphic arts

Peter Paul Rubens, *Study of Trees,* XVII century. Black chalk and brown ink, 58.2 x 48.9 cm
Honoré Daumier, *The Blacksmith,* XIX century. Lead pencil, black ink, grey wash with white highlights, 35.4 x 25.4 cm
Eugene Delacroix, pages from a notebook depicting travels in Morocco, 1832. Watercolour and graphite, 10.5 x 9.8 cm

Taken from life

A sketch broadly outlining a composition, a study of motion, a draft for a landscape, drawing comes in all forms. Even observations taken from life, such as those accompanying the impressions of Delacroix who, whilst travelling in Morocco, discovered a civilization: "Certain ancient everyday customs have a dignity which we are lacking under the gravest circumstances", he wrote in Tangiers on 28th April 1832. "The custom of the women of going to the graves with branches sold at the market. Engagements with music, the presents borne behind the relations, the couscous, the sacks of wheat on mules and donkeys, an ox, fabrics on cushions, etc. [...] They are closer to nature in a thousand ways: their dress, the shape of their shoes. Thus, there is beauty in everything they do. The rest of us, in our corsets, our tight shoes, our ridiculous girdles, we make a pitiful sight. Grace is wreaking revenge on our learning."

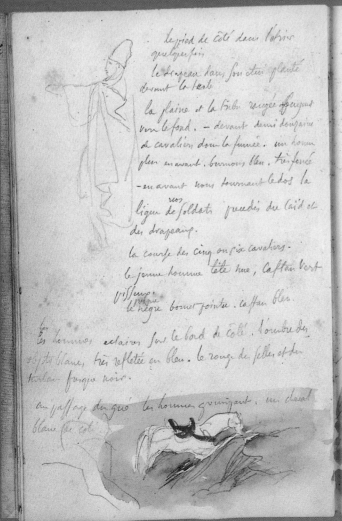

These works are located in the Richelieu wing, on the ground floor, in rooms 2, 5 and 10

French sculpture

Christ on the descent from the cross. Burgundy, c.1150. Wood with traces of gilding and polychromy, h: 155 cm
King Childebert. Paris, Abbey of Saint-Germain-des-Prés, 1239-1244. Stone with traces of polychromy, h: 191 cm
Tomb of Philippe Pot. Cîteaux, abbey-church, c.1475. Polychrome stone, h: 182 cm

Roman and gothic

Why do we talk today of "Roman art" and "Gothic art" when these expressions were never used during the Medieval period and do not correspond with any reality? It was during the last century that scholars dubbed as "Roman" the art of the early Middle Ages in reference to the Romance languages derived from Vulgar Latin. As far as the word "Gothic" is concerned, its history is one of the most complex: for, with the Renaissance, all medieval creations were called "Gothic", in other words, created by the Goths, by a "barbarian" people - considered uncivilized. The art of the Middle Ages was a strange sort of art, foreign and barbarian... Then people chose to consider that this Gothic had nothing of the Goth about it and drew for its source on Ile de France, in the middle of the XII century.

This work is located in the Richelieu wing, on the ground floor, in room 14 and in the Denon wing, Mollien staircase

French sculpture

Jean Goujon, *Nymph and Spirit,* Paris, Fontaine des Innocents, c.1547-1549. Stone, 73 x 195 cm
Benvenuto Cellini, *The Fontainebleau Nymph,* Anet, château of Diane de Poitiers, 1542-1543. Bronze, 205 x 409 cm

High style

In attracting to his palace at Fontainebleau Italian painters, sculptors, ornamenters and goldsmiths, Francis I established the first "Mannerist" centre in France and participated in the creation of a new style which favoured mythological themes, and was fond of free-flowing and slender lines. The whole of the XVI century would draw on this "first School of Fontainbleau". Maniera, as it was called during the Renaissance, or 'style', described the type of art which, moving away from nature, laid particular emphasis on virtuosity of form and graphic elegance, disproportioning and elongating bodies: the personification of grace, Jean Goujon's Nymph of the Fresh Waters splays her serpentine lines and her drenched raiments against the bas-relief of a fountain.

These works are located in the Marly Courtyard

French sculpture

Guillaume I Coustou, *Loose horse being restrained by a groom,* 1739-1745. Marble, h: 355 cm
The courtyard at Marly, with *Mercury astride Pegasus* and *Fame* Antoine Coysevox, 1699-1701

The king's horses

In 1679, Louis XIV erected, at Marly, a Sun pavilion and twelve small buildings, symbols of the twelve months of the year. As at Versailles, the architecture, garden and sculptures glorified the image of the sovereign, the omnipotent king, the warrior king and peacemaker. At the bend of waterfalls, fountains, ornamental lakes and clumps of trees stand sculptures to mythological subjects: thus, at the watering place, the winged horses of Antoine Coysevox depict Mercury and Fame. Forty years later, under the reign of Louis XV, they were followed by the equestrian groups of Guillaume Coustou. These were the dancing horses which adorned the place de la Révolution - nowadays the place de la Concorde - in 1795. Two centuries later, here they are at the Louvre.

These works are located in the Richelieu wing, on the ground floor in the Puget courtyard and in room 23

French sculpture

Edme Bouchardon, *Eros Carving his Bow from Hercules' Club,* 1739-1750. Marble, h: 173 cm
Antoine Louis Barye, *Lion with a Serpent,* 1832-1835. Bronze, h: 135 cm
Jean-Baptiste Pigalle, *Mercury Fastening his Winged Sandals,* 1744. Marble, h: 59 cm

Sculptors' techniques

Modelling in clay or wax, hewing from stone, moulding in plaster, casting in bronze: numerous are the techniques that make it possible to create a sculpture in the round, a high- or bas-relief, outline a form or undertake a monumental sculpture. In order to create a marble statue, the artist may work unaided and proceed to cut direct, attacking his material with points which rough-hew, gradines or chisels which form grooves, bush-hammers which flatten, rifflers which rasp and file... As for indirect cutting, this brings in sculptor's assistants: using a "perfecting machine" with a plumb line and a pair of compasses, they plot the measurements of a model against the final work. In such a case, the whole workshop is involved.

These works are located in the Denon wing,
on the ground floor, in room 4

Italian sculpture

Michelangelo Buonarroti, known as Michelangelo, *Slave,* or *The Dying Slave,*
1513-1515. Unfinished marble, h: 228 cm
Antonio Canova, *Psyche Revived by Cupid's Kiss,* 1793. Marble, h: 155 cm

The flesh of statues

Painter, sculptor, architect and poet, Michelangelo dazzled his contemporaries with his *terribilità*, his awesomeness, the power of his representation of the human body based on a consummate knowledge of anatomy. The writer Arétin paid tribute to this art in 1537: " With him, anatomy is transformed into music. With him, the human body is almost solely an architectonic form. In his frescoes and statues, the bodies are movements excelling themselves and the melodic lines of the muscles develop according to the laws of music, not those of representation. " Two centuries later, such were not the aesthetics of Canova, the adept of soft and languid flesh: " I could never understand what you call, with Michelangelo, anatomical knowledge. I think, for my part, that he deliberately strove for poses twisted in motion in order to accentuate, with excessive vehemence, the parts and muscles that most stand out. "

These works are located in the Richelieu wing,
on the 1st floor, in rooms 2, 3 and 4

Objets d'art

Liturgical Ewer, or Suger Eagle. Egypt or Imperial Rome, before 1147. Treasury of the Abbey of Saint-Denis. Porphyry, gilded and nielloed silver, h: 43.1 cm
Descent from the cross. Paris, c.1260-1280. Ivory with gilding and traces of polychromy
Sceptre of Charles V. (detail) Paris, 1364-1380. Treasury of the Abbey of Saint-Denis. Gold formerly enamelled, pearls and precious stones, h: 60 cm
Equestrian statuette of Charlemagne. Carolingian art, IX century. Treasury of Metz Cathedral. Bronze with traces of gilding, h: 23.5 cm
Reliquary-statuette, or Virgin with child by Jeanne d'Évreux (detail). Paris, between 1324 and 1339. Treasury of the Abbey of Saint-Denis. Gilded silver, translucent enamels on basse-taille, gold, rock crystal, pearls and precious stones, h: 69 cm

Treasuries

Cathedrals and abbeys often possess a "treasury", a place where precious objects, liturgical objects or saints' relics are kept. These items of silverware and gold work absolutely must be sumptous, outstanding and prestigious: for according to Father Suger who, in the XII century, devoted all his attention to embellishing Saint-Denis, such marvels make it possible for the faithful person to "pass from the material to the immaterial".

These works are located in the Richelieu wing,
on the 1st floor, in rooms 21-24

Objets d'art

Léonard Limosin, painted enamels. Limoges, middle of the XVI century.
In the centre: portrait of the High Constable Anne de Montmorency, 1556.
Painted enamel on copper, gilded wood mounting, h: 72 cm
School of Bernard Palissy, rustic-style bowl. France, c.1560. Enamelled terracotta,
52.5 x 40.2 cm
Massèot Abaquesne, altar step of the château of La Bâtie d'Urfé. Rouen, 1557.
Earthenware, L: 326 cm

Ceramics and enamel-firing

Whether it is earthenware, painted enamels or enamelled ceramics, ceramics and enamel-firing is one of
the most delicate of arts. Bernard Palissy testifies to this in his *Discours admirables* in 1580: " When I invented the method of making objects in the rustic style, I was even more troubled and anxious as a result than
before. For, having made a number of rustic-style bowls and fired them, some of my enamels were beautiful
and well-blended, others badly blended, others were burnt because they were made from different materials
that were fusible at different degrees. "

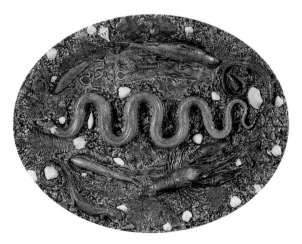

These works are located in the Denon wing,
on the 1st floor, in room 66

Objets d'art

Coronation crown of Louis XV. Paris, studio of Claude Rondé, start of the XVIII century. Treasury of the Abbey of Saint-Denis. Plate, gilded silver, reproduction of precious stones and embroidered satin
The Regent. Diamond discovered in India in 1698, cut in England at the start of the XVIII century. 140.64 metric carats
French school (XIX century). The Apollon galery at the Louvre museum (detail) cirea 1880. Oil on canvas, 460 x 550 cm

History of a diamond

Acquired in 1717 by Philippe of Orléans who left it his title, the "Regent" has passed from crown to crown, adorning those of Louis XV and Louis XVI, embellishing the hilt of the sword of the First Consul and then the blade of Napoleon I, even the diadem of the Empress Eugénie. Admired for its water - that translucidity and purity characteristic of precious stones -, famous for the cut given to it by an English craftsman who polished and facetted the jewel, it displays none of the faults, imperfections, marks or other defects referred to by diamond cutters as "crapauds", "gendarmes" and "jardinages" (blemishes and flaws).

These works are located in the Sully wing,
on the 1st floor, in room 34 and 64

Objets d'art

Charles Cressent, monkey commode. Paris, c.1735-1740. Made from deal and oak, satinwood and purple-heart veneer, gilded bronze and marble, h: 90 cm
Martin Carlin, Mme. du Barry's commode. Paris, second half of the XVIII century. Marquetry, plaques of Sèvres porcelain and gilded bronze
André Charles Boulle, wardrobe. Paris, c. 1700. Made from oak, ebony and tortoiseshell veneer, brass, tin, horn and coloured wood marquetry, gilded bronze, h: 260 cm
The great drawing-room of the duc de Morny, minister of Napoleon III, 1856-1861

Cabinet-making

"There is nothing that more denotes the magnificence of the grand princes than their superb palaces and the precious furniture with which they are adorned": with these words, Louis XIV in 1663 marked the founding of the royal furniture depository, thus acknowledging the importance of the craftsmen of wood who strove for his prestige. The word "cabinet-maker", which entered the language in 1676, describes someone who, unlike the carpenter, has become a master in the art of veneering and marquetry, blending with exotic or rare essences ebony, mahogany, rosewood or citron wood, horn, brass, copper or tin... If the materials varied, the same thing applied to the shape of the furniture; after chests and cupboards came the commode: for what is more commodious than this piece of furniture with drawers, it was exclaimed in 1705.

These works are located in the Denon wing,
Porte des Lions

World sculptures

Müyü ne bu: magic stone used for buying-castrated male pigs. Vanuatu, north of Ambrym Island, 18th early 19th century. volcarie tuff, h:35,5 cm
Seated male figure, orebok: "spirit", "dead". Guinée-Bissau, Caravela Island (Bissagos Archipelago), Bidjogo culture, 18th(?)-early 19th century. Yellow wood, red ochre marks, and inlaid lead in one eye, h: 37.7 cm
Tukah: royal mask. Western Cameroon, Bamileke Plateau, Bamendou Kingdom, first half of the 19th century. Wood, h: 86 cm
Moai kavakava: "male statuette with ribs". Easter Island, 17th(?)-18th century. Wood, obsidian and bone, h: 30 cm
Male head: portrait of a servant (?). South-west Nigeria, Yoruba country, Ife culture, 12th-14th century. Baked clay, h: 15.5 cm

Africa, Asia, Oceania, the Americas

"I experienced my greatest artistic emotion upon suddenly discovering the sublime beauty of sculptures created by anonymous African artists. These rig-orously logical and passionately sacred works are the most powerful and beautiful creations of the human imagination." Such were the words of Pablo Picasso quoted by Guillaume Apollinaire. When, at the beginning of the 20th century, Giacometti, Matisse, Brancusi, Lipchitz, Picasso and so many others found themselves faced with works originating from Oceania, the Americas, Asia and Africa, they were filled with immense admiration.